ON ROADS TO THE [illegible] CHRIST

ON ROADS TO THE HEALING CHRIST

by
BERT JORDAN

Published by
ARTHUR JAMES LIMITED
THE DRIFT, EVESHAM, WORCS.
WR11 4NW

First Edition 1976

ISBN 085305 187 9

SCRIPTURE SOURCES

Scripture references are taken from the New English Bible, Second Edition © 1970 by kind permission of Oxford and Cambridge University Presses

MADE AND PRINTED IN GREAT BRITAIN BY PURNELL AND SONS LTD.
PAULTON (AVON) AND LONDON

DEDICATION

To

MY WIFE

With love and gratitude for constant encouragement and willing involvement which have enriched my healing work beyond measure.

HEALING HANDS

JESUS, Lord and Friend and Healer—
Hands so human yet divine;
When you came as Heav'n's revealer
Touched not then this head of mine.
Risen Lord now
Rest upon us
Healing hands. The Kingdom's sign.

Small hands clasped in boyhood wonder
Temple teachers sit in awe!
Seeking then your Father's bidding—
Young heart straining to His call.
Hands that pray are
Hands of healing. . . .
Let them rest upon us all.

Youthful hands in duty fashioned
Wood and nail for yoke and plough.
Youthful heart with love empassioned,
Longed to fashion heart and soul.
Hands that work are
Hands of healing. . . .
Let them rest upon us now.

Hands that beckoned twelve disciples—
Called from toil to heal and bless;
Hands upheld in benediction
On so many in distress.
Hands that beckon
Us to follow. . . .
Lovingly our heads caress.

Hands at eventide were laid on
Many who were sick and blind;
  Touching them to vital living—
Healed in body, soul and mind.
      Hands of love are
      Hands of healing. . . .
Rest them, Lord, on all mankind.

We in spirit lowly kneeling
See the Risen Lord. He stands
  Still with loving care revealing
Wondrous pow'r in healing hands.
      Countless blessings
      Freely given. . . .
In our midst the Master stands.

Bert Jordan

FOREWORD
by
R. W. Hugh Jones, B.A.
Provincial Moderator of the United Reformed Church

I AM IMMENSELY GLAD this book has been written. It would be idle to pretend that the ministry of healing is now accepted as part of the Church's life and work by all who are called Christians. Many still fail to see this as one of the significant factors among the signs of renewal in the Church now. Unhappily it has been given a distorted image by activities with little claim to be a demonstration of the power of Christ to heal in our time as surely as He healed the sick during His ministry in Galilee and Judea. It is good, therefore, to have the evidence this book provides.

No one who knows him, and who has lived close to his ministry, can doubt that Bert Jordan is an instrument of the healing power of Christ. Many of us are glad that he has now agreed to set down on paper something of his experience. By this means an uncounted number who do not know him personally may come to know something of his mind and conviction in the territory of human need and the answer to it which Christ Himself can give. The writer offers his own prayer in the book: "I pray that many who do not know Him intimately may be led to discover Him in these pages." I have not the slightest doubt that that prayer will be answered.

FOREWORD

In the broken condition of the world now we are asked to listen to so many voices offering negative messages. Personally and corporately men and women urgently need the sound of a voice which will give positive assurance of a power which can make us whole again. That voice may be heard here by all who will make themselves ready to listen.

I am glad to have the privilege of writing this Foreword. It gives me the opportunity to set on record my own gratitude to Bert Jordan for his ministry. I commend this book with all my heart.

HUGH JONES

Kenilworth, 1976

PREFACE

WHETHER OR NOT this book was written under the Holy Spirit's prompting is not for me to say, but I believe it was. Certainly it was undertaken as a result of the pressures of friends and colleagues who are aware of the way God has blessed the healing work which has proved so enriching a part of my ministry. Some who urged its writing have themselves been healed. Many have shared the experiences recorded here. Where I quote actual cases, they are mainly from written or taped statements from the people concerned and are included with their permission.

This book does not press theological arguments for the continuing work of healing that Christ made so vital a part of His earthly ministry. It speaks of the experiences that have led a very ordinary working minister to a deep enrichment of his pastoral care in which his own people and many others have shared. It is therefore written with humility and thankfulness. It could not be otherwise, for there are few experiences so humbling and so full of joy as to meet again those who have been healed.

In thankfulness to God, this ministry is commended with all my heart.

There are well-known roads on which the Christ was discovered in New Testament days. The Damascus Road where Saul kicked against the prodding of the Holy Spirit until he was confronted on that rebellious road by the risen Lord. Some have walked that road reluctant to believe that the healing ministry is meant to be part of our commitment.

The Emmaus Road has a word for the disappointed whose despair leads them out of the battle. In the very act of giving up, hearts are strangely warmed as the risen Lord overtakes us.

The Jericho Road speaks clearly of human need and the opportunity to meet that need. We may pass by on the other side, not because we are unwilling to help but because our faith does not always equal our compassion.

The Road of Assurance is a personal road on which many have thankfully travelled. Here we have known that healing touch for ourselves or others. New Testament roads tell thrilling stories, but we do not live in the first century. We walk the familiar roads of our day and they need not be dull and commonplace, for we journey with the same Lord who walked the lanes of Galilee. To discover that Divine Companion, fills modern roads with new purpose and we know a power beyond our own.

This book is written with the prayer that it may encourage the doubtful to search until he finds the Christ who still heals and blesses. This leads, as it must, to the practical road of a glad assurance of partnership with God. Roads of challenge and discovery, of opportunity and partnership, are not distant highways covered with the dust of history, but the familiar roads where we live.

On the roads of common Christian duty and faithful commitment, the Healing Christ is still to be found, for He belongs not only to the New Testament but also to the daily life of ordinary men and women.

If twentieth-century Christianity is to have impact on this age it must not be merely an account of the Christ who once lived among men, but a positive, life-changing encounter with a risen Lord. A Lord still active in human affairs and still leading that mission of healing and redemption. We do not worship a dead hero but a living Lord.

A friend and colleague after a rapid loss of weight was admitted to hospital where examination showed a growth or blockage in the bowel. A further X-Ray on the day before the proposed operation revealed it plainly. A prayer with the laying-on-of-hands brought a sense of peace and a night's good sleep. When the surgeon operated the next day it was discovered that there was now no trace of the growth. The patient was soon well again.

Many such stories can be thankfully told of this ministry which is part of the Church's continuing work.

Be assured that on modern roads and in the place where you live and work, "His touch has still its ancient power."

BERT JORDAN

Wolverhampton

CONTENTS

1

A ROAD OF DISCOVERY

ANY BOOK on the Church's Ministry of Healing is likely to ask more questions than it answers. This book is no exception. What questions it does seek to answer will be from a growing assurance of experience and personal conviction. Not a very satisfactory source of answer maybe, but assuring enough to keep the writer, an ordinary working minister, to the task to which he feels called—the preaching of the Word and the healing of the sick in the name of Christ.

The word "assuring" may be too strong for all occasions, for there are moments when faith seems little more than doubts kept quiet. It may be that some such moments are good for us, for a humble spirit is needed in prayer. It is not we who heal, but God. Most of us know how self-assurance can so easily shade into pride and get in the way of our usefulness. It can block channels that nothing but humility can keep open.

Jesus was on the Mount of Transfiguration while some of His disciples were left in the valley. They learned to their discomfiture that without Him they could do nothing. A distracted father brought his son to be healed. Jesus was not there but the disciples were. They could manage! They tried but knew the humiliation of failure, for the boy remained unhealed. With the arrival of Jesus new hope came to the father and his son was healed. The disciples needed this lesson. Still baffled by their failure and unaware of what was wrong, they sought Jesus out privately and asked Him, "Why could not we cast it out?" (Mark 9: 28). We have asked that same question in our disappointments and have been given the same answer, "There is no means of casting out this sort but prayer."

This ministry can be a costly one and part of the cost is an honest self-effacement. We soon learn that channels must be kept open and this is one of the disciplines we must obey. To be sure it is not enough, for we need to bring faith and compassion and a longing to help. It is still true that humility is an important first step on the road to the discovery of healing power.

This is not an argument for a specialised ministry. It tells of the enriching power of such a work as it becomes an integral part of the Church's life. Its demands are many but its joys are evident as a minister, in the midst of many duties, serves his people in this intimate way. This is where human need is so much in evidence and this is where the risen Lord still walks to meet that need. It is based on happy partnership in which pastoral work takes on a new dimension. The power available cannot be argued but can be experienced. The encouragement of a prayer group adds something indefinable to pastoral caring and we shall discuss this more fully in a later chapter.

One thing is certain. While still on the road of discovery, men and women are healed and brought to a newness of life. The Christ is seen to be so close to human need, a part of every situation and so lovingly involved. Sometimes healing is immediate, sometimes it takes time. We should co-operate by our patience as well as by our faith. Physical healings take place with startling results. I have ministered to a woman whose thumb joint was swollen with arthritis and which could not be even slightly touched without pain. To hold that hand gently in the presence of Christ banished the pain and the thumb went down to normal size under our eyes.

The need often arises to minister to those disturbed in mind and spirit. Prayer can be so effective as hands are laid on troubled heads. The change is clearly seen. Anxieties are lifted and fears subside and a sense of freedom is felt as the Christ heals.

A young woman, very unwell and under psychiatric treatment, was brought to my Vestry Hour by a friend who had herself known healing a year or two before. The sorrow on that young face was unmistakable, for her fears were deeply rooted, but after prayer, in which the nearness of the Lord was wonderfully sensed, her eyes lit up with a new light. As she left us that night she said simply, "I never thought I should ever be able to smile again."

There are those whose need includes the healing of a situation of tension or unhappiness. Healing prayer brings refreshment to the spirit and an experience of the peace of God, even when physical healing is delayed or hindered by reasons we may not yet understand.

Questions? Of course there are questions! More questions than answers with our present knowledge, but this ministry is fruitful to a degree that makes its worth evident. The problem of failure is a real one, but apparent "failures" do not deny the power of God, for we are privileged to see so much to the contrary. Some will tell us that if God heals there should be no failures. They forget that no part of the Christian outreach is all victory. Not everyone who hears the Gospel is converted. Thank God for those who know a life-changing experience as the Word is preached, but we do not give up proclaiming that Word because this does not always happen. Even our Lord knew that much of what He said fell like seed on stony ground.

In many discussions on the healing ministry, I have heard ministers confess to an inward hope to have part in it. When this longing is felt a man should grasp it with all his might. Let him bring faith and compassion and courage to it and God will surely use him. I shall always be grateful to a colleague who once said that to me. We are not forgetting the part that the non-ordained may play in this work. It is a vital part. A minister, by his very calling, is closely in touch with his people and will know better than most the deep need for their wholeness. The stress of modern living proves too much for so many, and a disturbing percentage of our fellows need medical and psychiatric care. The need for a firm anchorage of faith in the Healing Christ is plainly seen.

To lead men and women to such an assurance and to witness the healing work of Christ in them is a moving and profound experience. Conversations often turn to story after story of unaccountable answers to prayer. Very few Christians will deny that God breaks into human situations with a power beyond our understanding. It is an impoverished faith that knows no such moments. Such experiences keep us mindful of our need of prayer and prod us to look again at the promises of the Gospel. Jesus meant what He said: "He who has faith in me will do what I am doing; and he will do greater things still because I am going to the Father. Indeed anything you ask in my name I will do, so that the Father may be glorified in the Son. If you ask anything in my name I will do it" (John 14: 12-14).

It is a matter of common humanity to comfort the sick and troubled and the Christian faith equips us for this. True enough, many without such a faith can do so. Comfort is not enough and the Gospel promises so much more. No one will deny the encouragement of words that cheer, but most of us know moments when words are not enough and where mere advice seems almost unkind.

On my own road of discovery the sense of shame and dissatisfaction I felt seemed to be the prompting of the Holy Spirit. Horizons widened as obedience to that prompting opened up a ministry for which I thank God. When some needs are left unmet the fault may be ours. Unused power and unclaimed promises shame us as we realise that we might have made profound discoveries had we been willing to undertake the disciplines involved. No man is satisfied with being less than he need be.

The pastoral demands of the full-time ministry are more exacting than many would believe. If the "care of the flock" is no more than a duty it will be physically exhausting, for listening takes more from you than talking does. Frustration in this field can lead to even less effective pastoral care. Some barriers must go before useful work can be done and attitudes that hinder need radical change. See how we become embarrassed when we try to get to the heart of the matter. This is shameful and tragic.

I once went into the home of an ex-deacon who was gravely ill and I was told by his wife to keep the conversation general and on no account to pray with him as he would realise how ill he was! This in a Christian home where it should be the most natural thing in the world to ask God's help in time of trouble. Every minister knows what it is to make a home-visit and be aware of some deep problem yet, in the presence of the family, be unable to get to the point. The television is either left on or the conversation gets no further than the weather or the latest cricket score.

It was because of such situations that I felt the urgent need to be available at some set time each week so that my people (and others) should have the opportunity of sharing things they so needed to discuss. There are some situations that can rapidly deteriorate if no such opportunities are given.

Don't let it be misunderstood, for I believe that visits to the homes of his people can be rewarding to the minister who will see the privilege of it. It can lead to "mountain-top" experiences to come as a friend into the familiar surroundings of home or garden. Being on their own ground can sometimes mean a self-assurance that enables our people to open up more than might be possible in the formal atmosphere of the vestry. Both methods are needful for they complement each other. The important thing is to be aware of another's need and be willing to share it. There is undoubted value in wise and sympathetic counselling providing it does not become a human contribution which leaves out the fact of an active and healing Lord.

It was the knowledge of my own inadequacy that sent me, ashamed and hurt in spirit, back to the New Testament and the wrestling prayer that cried out for an answer. To be called to administer the Word and Sacraments must surely carry with it the promise of power beyond our own. Who otherwise can serve his people's deepest needs? We can do nothing without the Lord's help, though we try hard enough!

There is a social side of helpfulness that I would not belittle. To fetch groceries or bring in a bucket of coal, to prepare a meal or sit with the lonely are services the Lord will bless. But this is not *all* that can be done. The promises of Christ are so much richer and more alive with His re-creative power. Clearly seen in His earthly days, and clearly seen today as His touch brings healing of body and mind and spirit.

Who would dare limit the purpose of His coming to earth? The revelation of God's great plans for mankind and the purpose of human destiny that surges from His Father-heart are the eternal themes. With so few years allowed Him for that tremendous work, He found time to deal with individuals in a way which made clear their eternal worth. He spoke to an immoral woman by a well at noonday and found time to listen to a man who came secretly to Him at midnight. He journeyed to heal a sick child. All this and much more made it plain that God is a Father to His children and none is outside His care.

This was the good news His disciples were to preach. News of a Kingdom of wholeness in which men and women are healed and made new and the individual takes on an importance because he is the temple of the living God. Coupled with that Gospel went the healing of the sick. As Jesus healed, so His disciples were given orders to lay hands upon the sick in His name. It is a simple fact of experience that in obedience to that command Jesus heals today through His dedicated servants.

Reach this point if you can, and see the need for Church and minister to be assured that we are never in any situation alone. If Jesus is mistaken here, the Gospel makes nonsense. In prayer that makes us ready to receive we can be sure of the response that can make our faith throb with meaning. So much is open to us if we have faith enough in a Divine Companion. Limited results in a ministry that was so largely self-reliant set me on my own road of discovery on which, by the grace of God, prayer came alive and opened up acres of the pastoral field that were once fallow.

In following chapters we look at some of the events that took place on New Testament roads and discover the same Lord healing on the familiar roads of today. His compassionate power still meets human need.

I was in the Christian ministry for many years before it even occurred to me that God would bless so personal and intimate a work as that which the Healing Christ makes possible. I was certainly unaware of possessing any of the qualities that one would suspect the Lord would need. True, I look back on answered prayer with the wisdom that comes after the event. Though I did not realise it, the Lord was already leading me in this work of prayer and healing.

I called on an elderly woman whose arthritis had troubled her for fourteen years. She had been confined to her bed for some years and was in constant pain. It was not possible for her to lift a cup of tea to her lips. We talked for a bit and then I prayed with her, putting my hand on her arm. She called me back to the bedside as I was leaving and said, "When you touched my arm, the pain went." Further visits brought relief from pain and the strength to get up. It was with great delight that she showed how she could now lift a cup of tea above the level of her head on to a high mantelpiece. It was this experience and a growing uneasiness about the effectiveness of pastoral work that led me, under God, to seek a more positive way.

So it was that my search really began in 1955 in the early days of my pastorate at Rubery, on the Worcestershire border of the city of Birmingham. I was on a road to discovery for which I can never be grateful enough.

Two steps seemed important. The first was that my wife and I made ourselves available at a set time each week to meet our people. We soon realised that others from outside of our own fellowship found value in what we were doing. We met in the vestry at the church and it became known as "The Vestry Hour", though it soon extended beyond that time. I was convinced of its ultimate usefulness, but the start of it was a discipline of patience, for it must have been three months before anyone came for healing prayer.

Once begun the work continued and soon extended far beyond the local church and district. It is still a vital part of the Church's outreach, continuing through pastorates in Castleford, Yorkshire, and in Wolverhampton where, set in the heart of an immigrant area, the Church finds many opportunities of serving the community, none more fruitful than proclaiming the Healing Christ.

The Vestry Hour shares in prayer for those who come in sickness or trouble. Part of its value lies in its regularity. People feel free to come as often as they wish until the time comes when we can thank God together for the healing of mind or body or the repairing of a situation. In prayer and the laying-on-of-hands there is always an inward healing of the spirit. There is a welcome by my wife as they arrive, when her quiet, relaxed attitude sets the right atmosphere. Sharing with others in the small waiting room proves helpful. Those who know healing for themselves bring others, and over the years we thank God for the friendships we have made and for the scores of men and women who find the Christ who is faithful to His promises. It is a deep joy to meet them again after many years. Some have told their stories which are quoted throughout this book.

Together with the Vestry Hour, a second development widened the contribution the Church itself could make. I gathered a group of interested people and formed a Prayer and Healing Study Group. Those who began this study and preparation were soon committed to it and there was a loyalty that is not always achieved in other parts of the Church's work. We studied the New Testament and looked with new eyes upon the healing work of our Lord. A library of books on healing taught us a good deal of the experience of others.

After two years the pattern changed as members were committed to the work and some had themselves been healed. We changed the name to "The Prayer and Healing Fellowship" and it became more devotional in nature. There were prayers for those on a prayer-list and ministries to any who felt the need. I have never since been without the support of such a group and know the undeniable value of it. Certain it is that such a group soon discovers a power beyond itself as it draws upon Divine resources. Prayer becomes more positive and meaningful with the added strength that comes when men and women pray together with a common mind and purpose.

Through Vestry Hour and group discussion the road widens and the way becomes clearer. There are some misty patches and the way is not always clearly defined, but at least we are on a highway and not in some uncharted moorland. It becomes the road of discovery.

This book will have served its purpose if it encourages others to step out on that road which will enrich their way as mine has been enriched. The need is obvious. The living water is ours for the asking, but we need to come to it thirsty.

2

THE JERICHO ROAD

TWO FAMILIAR STORIES have their setting on the Jericho road. One is the well-known parable. During my war service in the Tank Corps, before I entered the ministry, I met many who could not say the Lord's Prayer. Some had no idea why Christians celebrated Whitsuntide, but I never met anyone who had not heard the story of the Good Samaritan.

It told of a common enough occurrence in the days of Jesus when patrolling by the occupying Romans could not prevent every outbreak of lawlessness. Even today thieves may get away in spite of motorway patrols and the speedy communications of short-wave radio. There are modern Jericho roads where travellers are left wounded by the roadside. The Christ still needs the Samaritan with compassion and courage enough to lend a hand.

There is so much that challenges us to action as we realise the vast area of human need. It is so widespread and life goes wrong as tensions build up in the kind of life we live in a modern world. We note the problems of alcoholism and drug addiction and the alarming percentage of those who require psychiatric treatment. Then we realise that we are not talking of problems but of people! Men and women from our office or living just up the road from us, wounded by stresses that prove too much for them, and in dire need of Samaritan help.

The sheer size of the task tempts us to by-pass its challenge. We agree with Studdert Kennedy's suggestion that the Samaritan was lucky, for he found only one man on the Jericho road. He had the oil and the wine and the money to pay the innkeeper. *We* find so many on the roads of today and, however strongly our Christian conscience challenges us, we have not always got the wine and oil or the money to pay the landlord. No minister that I know is able to deal adequately with all the pastoral demands even of his own parish. Human inadequacy forces us back on Him who promised grace sufficient for our need and the power to do the impossible.

In the healing partnership that our Lord offers, help can be given in a way that nothing but faith and obedience will make possible. This is encouraging and can be the needed antidote to the inadequacy that keeps us immobile. Of course there are other ways in which the Church travels its Jericho roads and shares the comfort of the Gospel. In many practical ways the Church accepts the challenge to action. It is tempting to pass by on the other side, for involvement is time-consuming and inconvenient. We may take a closer look as the Levite did and still decide not to be involved. Whatever our response the choice is presented. Shall we close our eyes and pretend that it is none of our business, or do what we can to be a ministering Samaritan?

The Gospel is clear. *We are not limited to human resources.* The command to preach the Gospel and heal the sick includes a promised "power" and an unseen Companion. I know of no privilege more profound than to bring someone, hurt and wounded, into the care and compassion of our Lord in the faith that He will share the situation. His healing grace can reach wounds too deep for any other kind of surgery and is a wholeness that covers all our need. It is not enough, for example, to free the arthritic from pain yet leave some possible bitterness unhealed.

Every minister can tell of answered prayer that has enriched his own ministry. Many would be encouraged in a wider healing work if they had the support of a praying and caring group within their churches. This is not a criticism, but a challenge to the many good layfolk in our churches who could serve in this way. Based on scripture it is part of the full obedience to which we are all called. James writes to that early Christian community in his fifth chapter, "Is anyone among you in trouble? He should turn to prayer. Is anyone in good heart? He should sing praises. Is one of you ill? He should send for the elders of the congregation to pray over him and anoint him with oil in the name of the Lord. A good man's prayer is powerful and effective" (James 5: 13-16).

Too few are ready to obey this scriptural injunction; and as a consequence we miss the way and fail one another. Living close to our Lord's promised presence makes a group of Christians into a therapeutic community. There is a wonderful reality about the moment of ministry in which we feel His touch upon us. Prayer must not be a half-hearted hope or a nagging uncertainty and it will not be if we trust the healing Lord to fulfil His word. Results may be startling and healing can be complete. This is demonstrated so often in the midst of a faithful group who pray for the troubled.

Listen to one who knew, not only physical healing, but

a lasting assurance of a new-found Lord: "For months I have suffered severe pain in my legs and, as my work made it necessary for me to be on my feet all day, it was a great trial to me. At the suggestion of a friend I went to the Prayer and Healing Fellowship led by the Rev. Bert Jordan. I received the laying-on-of-hands with the prayer that pain might be removed and that I be made whole. That week I had one attack of pain which proved to be the last, for it never returned. I received another ministry the next week and again the following week and continued to attend the Prayer Fellowship. Bodily healing is not all that I received. I have come to experience a Lord who is so real in a personal way that I have never known before. It is as though I have found an assurance I have been looking for all my life."

The healing of Christ includes the whole of us. Physical healing is never enough in itself. Attitudes and situations can be transformed as we are set on a road of glad discovery.

Those who know the despair of being unable to cope with life can be uplifted in the atmosphere of healing love. In such a group they sense that people care. Breakdown conditions can be frightening and so little understood by others who have never known it themselves or in the family. Most of us meet with it sometime, if only in a friend or neighbour. As a Free Church chaplain in a psychiatric hospital, and in the healing work of the pastorate, I find it common enough. The joy of seeing someone freed from depression cannot be described, yet healing in this sphere is undoubted.

A young girl beset with irrational fears received a ministry during a stay in hospital and, on her discharge, came for further help to my church. The journey was on two 'bus routes across the city of Birmingham. This she did regularly long after she was healed, for she became a valued member of the prayer group. Occasionally some of the old fears returned but were quickly banished in prayer and she was well again. She has been happily married for some years. Many need the anchor of faith so often demonstrated within a dedicated group. Like a ship that rides at anchor, a shared faith keeps us steady until the waters are calmer.

The warning from the lips of Jesus is relevant to the Jericho roads we travel. "I tell you this: anything you did for one of my brothers here, however humble, you did for me" (Matt. 25: 40). On the Jericho roads of this twentieth century, British social services give us access to the wine and the oil and the donkey, but this does not obviate the caring compassion that goes beyond the mere fact of provision. Then, too, Christian men and women know the "Innkeeper" to whom we may bring with confidence those for whom the journey has proved too much.

* * * *

The second story of the Jericho road is not a parable but an event. It happened as Jesus and His disciples left the city. Jesus had told of what would happen to Him in Jerusalem, a city notorious for its rejection of the prophets. Now they leave Jericho on the Jerusalem road and Jesus heals a blind beggar. ". . . As He was leaving the town, with His disciples and a large crowd, Bartimaeus son of Timaeus, a blind beggar, was seated at the roadside. Hearing that it was Jesus of Nazareth, he began to shout, 'Son of David, Jesus, have pity on me!' Many of the people told him to hold his tongue; but he shouted all the more, 'Son of David, have pity on me.'

Jesus stopped and said, 'Call him'; so they called the blind man and said, 'Take heart; stand up; he is calling you.' At that he threw off his cloak, sprang up, and came to Jesus. Jesus said to him, 'What do you want me to do for you?' 'Master,' the blind man answered, 'I want my sight back.' Jesus said to him, 'Go; your faith has cured you.' And at once he recovered his sight and followed him on the road" (Mark 10: 46-52).

This story is crammed with lessons as it lives and throbs with meaning and takes you from the realms of theory down to the practical. A matter-of-fact record of a very un-matter-of-fact event. A blind beggar. One of thousands who seemed destined to go through life denied the self-respect of earning his own living. Who among us can imagine his situation? The Sioux Indians have a proverb that they must judge no man until they have walked for six weeks in his moccasins. Who can really understand what it was to a Bartimaeus, to beg for bread because no one would employ him? On the same road in which a man fell among thieves this man relied on the generosity of passers-by.

We are all "beggars" who rely on the generosity of others, for no one is self-sufficient. "Blessed are they who know they are poor. The kingdom of God is theirs." With the sharpened senses of the unsighted, Bartimaeus would no doubt have heard the conversations of those who walked past. Some would claim that Jesus was a prophet; some would say that He mixed with the strangest company and was a friend of sinners. There would be those who derided His claims, pointing out that He was a carpenter's son who ran foul of the authorities, gathered a few uneducated fishermen around Him and got them on some mad mission about a coming kingdom. It was on Jesus as a healer that Bartimaeus would set his hopes.

A friend of mine, whose story follows, put her faith in His healing power. She attended a meeting at which I spoke of the healing ministry and went away determined to believe that the Christ would help if she was ever in such need. She little knew how soon it would be before her faith was tried. Listen to her own words: "I have worn glasses since childhood, my left eye in particular being very weak. With glasses my sight was good and I had no trouble until 1967. In the autumn of that year I began rapidly to lose the sight of my right eye. This was so serious that I could not read even the headlines of the newspaper with both eyes together. A specialist examined me and I underwent many tests. I was then told that the condition was chronic and that the rapid deterioration of my right eye was due to a fatty growth which was thought to be T.B. I was given no hope of a cure.

"Soon after this verdict I attended the Vestry Hour of the Rev. Bert Jordan and went expecting to be healed at once. There was no apparent improvement and yet I came away with faith undiminished. The following day—a Sunday—I did not attend church, for I could not have seen the numbers on the hymn-board. Later that day severe pain came to my right eye and I went to bed wishing I had never had the ministry. Imagine my joy the next morning to discover that I could read not only the headlines but the small print as well! Apart from a slight mist which cleared in a week or two, my sight was as good as ever.

"Although I still wear glasses, my eyesight is as good as ever as I write this, some five years after my healing.

A side effect of the eye trouble was severe headache which came periodically. I have not had such a headache since the day of the ministry."

A blind beggar healed on the Jericho road in the days of Jesus and a young married woman healed in the twentieth century—both restored and blessed by the same Lord. We are still on roads with the Healing Christ.

Think for a moment of those who were with Jesus when Bartimaeus was healed. They had part in what happened, for without the babble of conversation Jesus might have passed by unheard. They would remember that day as long as they lived; and if, in later years, some scoffed at the story, they would be able to say, "But I was there when Bartimaeus received his sight."

Perhaps you have memories of a day when, because you walked with your Lord, someone in desperate need was able to meet Him. Never under-rate what Jesus can do through you. When you are tempted to doubt your usefulness, remember the crowd around Jesus as He left the city that day and the part they played in the healing of a man who could not see.

A surprising number of those who have known healing in my own ministry have been brought to it by friends. One such man came to the Vestry Hour at the invitation of a friend who had herself been healed. He was an ex-guardsman with the stature needed for that profession. At the time he sought healing he had lost so much weight that he was seven stone eight and a half pounds instead of his normal weight of fourteen stone.

He had a thyroid condition of some five years standing and was very ill indeed. His eyes were swollen to such an extent that he could not shut them at all, and a heart attack brought a pulse rate of 128. His weight continued to drop over many months and his knees were locked in a bent position so that he could not walk. He affirms that he was told he would never walk again. From the first ministry he stopped losing weight and each week as he came for prayer he built up until he regained his original weight. Within six months of his first ministry he was advised to diet and get down to twelve stone. A ministry in his home brought freedom to locked knees and he walked freely again. I saw him some nine years after his healing to ask permission to include his story in this book. He was fit and well at the age of 67. He stood in front of the fireplace and lifted each leg in turn and stood with perfect steadiness on one leg.

He met the Healing Christ because someone who walked with her Lord made that introduction possible.

See the contrast in some who stood near to Bartimaeus that day when Jesus came by. They told him to keep quiet! They might have confirmed the blind man's hope that it was Jesus coming his way, but they were sure that He would not want to be bothered with a blind beggar. How wrong they were! God forgive us for the faithlessness that misreads His compassion. A woman came to seek prayer in my Vestry Hour. She was very unwell and told me that her minister had told her that we have no right to pray for healing, for we should bear sickness with patience. It may well be that many a modern Bartimaeus has remained unhealed because he has heeded the voice of someone whose insensitive spirit could never lead another to the place where Christ can bless.

Notice the change of attitude in those who stood near

to Bartimaeus that day. Jesus heard the note of faith and urgency in the blind man's voice. "Call him," He said. They no longer told him to keep quiet. "Take heart," they said. "Stand up; He is calling you." Attitudes that are negative need to be changed to positive, for undoubtedly our attitudes can either help or hinder.

I ministered to a patient in a large city hospital and walked down the ward with the specialist who was treating him. He spoke of his personal belief in healing prayer but pointed out that, because of their training and knowledge of the prognosis, it was not easy for the nursing staff to care for a dying man with positive hope for his recovery. This is understandable, and yet we need to remember that all things are possible with Christ. We are part of the continuing ministry of our Lord and in Him we have divine resources to draw upon if we have faith enough.

Thank God for every agency of healing and never be afraid of asking too much of a Lord who gave Himself for us. Never discourage another from asking and receiving that wondrous touch of Christ. Not—"Keep quiet—He is too busy to deal with you"—but, "Stand up; take heart; He is calling you."

3

THE EMMAUS ROAD

CLEOPAS AND A FRIEND whose name we do not know walked despondently along the road to Emmaus. They were going home. Having become involved in the mission of the young Galilean, they shared with many the hope that He was the Messiah. Those hopes were smashed as Jesus was led out to crucifixion. Maybe these two disciples had watched it all and had been with Him in earlier days; seen Him draw upon heavenly resources as He fed the multitude and healed the sick. Maybe they had hoped for some divine intervention right to the last minute, but at the end of that grim day their Lord had been laid in a borrowed tomb. So Cleopas and his companion went home. It was not until they invited Him in that they discovered who it was who had walked with them.

I wonder how many miles we travel unaware of that risen Lord? Certainly I travelled the road of my early ministry without realising that the Lord I served was still the Healing Christ, although many prayers had been answered through those years.

When I was very young in experience in the ministry, I was part-time chaplain to a T.B. sanatorium. Denomination counts little in hospital visits and one day I spoke to a young woman of a Church different from my own. She was very ill with pain in the spine that would not be eased. I later learned that she was feared to be near the end after a long illness. We talked of our Lord's compassion and prayed together. I had never ministered with the laying-on-of-hands before, and as I put my hands upon her it was not a conscious act, but rather a gesture of the compassion I felt. Her pain was eased as we prayed and within a few weeks she was able to go home. I do not even know her name.

This shows my own foolishness, for I still did not understand that this was part of the Church's healing work. That was my Emmaus road on which the Christ was surely my companion, but I had not reached the point of recognising that He was still the Healing Christ of the Gospels. Indeed it was five or six years later that I learned what he must have been trying to make clear that day.

On the Emmaus road we meet a risen Lord who keeps His word. He never disappoints. Without that conviction we may reach for a lofty morality and be inspired to a useful manhood, but not reach the point where we are sure of His touch upon us or the reality of His companionship. He must not remain the Christ of history but become the Lord of every day, friend as well as Saviour. A compassionate Lord so closely involved in human situations whom we can invite into our homes.

This may seem naive and childish, but it is not so. Not a childish faith that makes credulity a virtue but a childlike faith that will trust a father's love. On this road with Cleopas and his friend fears prove groundless and lost hopes are recovered and fulfilled. Not that this answers all our questions, but we can look with new insights at the New Testament picture of a Lord who meets our need as we experience His power in prayer.

What happened in the first century happens still. On modern roads we can rejoice in an unchanging Lord.

God the Creator and Father is made so clear in Jesus. Who was it who said, "If God is not like Jesus, He ought to be"? Be thankful that some conceptions of God no longer hold us captive. He is a Father of infinite love. Not soft and weak-charactered so that we become spoilt children who are not allowed to grow up to mature manhood. Neither is He an unfeeling, remote creator who torments us with disease and sorrow.

What nonsense is talked about the will of God! Vague and ill-founded ideas about Him encourage a curious contradiction of a Father who sends our sickness—and a Christ who heals it. I do not turn glibly aside from the thorny problem of a God who allows disease but does not send it. Whatever the truth is we must surely not allow a conflict between the compassionate work of Christ and the perfect will of His Father. It is a pseudo-piety that sees disease as God's will, yet does everything possible to get rid of it.

Our words give us away. "I suppose this is the will of God," is said by someone in some devastating sorrow but not said when things go well for us. Why only in misfortune do we ask, "What have I done to deserve this?" as if all unpleasant happenings are sent for punishment or discipline? What a sorrow we lay on that Father-heart by denying His compassion. God shares with us as Jesus did in His earthly life, to bless and heal and renew us. He wills our wholeness.

John Robinson's words to the Pilgrim Fathers, as they set out for a new world across the Atlantic, still have the ring of truth about them. "The Lord has more truth yet to break forth out of His holy word." That

Stranger who overtakes us on our Emmaus roads opens up the scriptures and we see the Creator as Jesus reveals Him. Man's conception of God's character has matured with the years. From early thought of a tribal god whose territorial limits were accepted, to faith in the one great Creator. From the punishing, vindictive God who gives command to kill and destroy, to Christ who loves us to the end and can say of His murderers, "Father, forgive them; they do not know what they are doing" (Luke 23: 34).

Look upon the Father as Jesus portrayed Him and it is evident that He never "wills" our sickness and disease. Jesus never missed an opportunity to fulfil His Father's will. No artist is satisfied with creative work that is less than his best. The imperfect never satisfies. How dare we suggest that the Creator deliberately creates His children malformed or incomplete? You cannot make sense of belief in a loving Father and at the same time see such dreadful limitation as the planned and deliberate purpose of God. It makes nonsense of the New Testament which, in the life and work of Jesus and the drama of Good Friday, shows a love and a compassion beyond our comprehension.

Prayer is not honest if you are convinced in advance that God will not respond. Positive praying is impossible unless you hope for an answer. It is difficult to pray with any realism until this issue is settled. "I tell you, then, whatever you ask for in prayer, believe that you have received it and it will be yours" (Mark 11: 24). To pray for someone to be healed and at the same time to believe—or half believe—that God wills his illness, is little more than a pious exercise, and not very pious at that! No Christian doctor could work under such conditions, for a Christian does not go against the will of God. If the Father really wills our sickness, what right have we to get rid of it? Let there be no nagging uncertainty about God's will as we pray for the sick.

The question is sometimes asked if we ought to pray for healing when, humanly speaking, the illness is terminal. We can never be sure that it is! Even so, a quiet passing into the next life may well be the final healing. Under prayer, pain can often be relieved and the valley of the shadow illuminated and the passing made peaceful. It would seem that in that moment of passing our Lord can be very near as we discover the truth of His promise to receive us.

Visits to a dear old couple brought many a quiet chat in which the wife told of her daily prayer that she would not be taken first, for her husband would not manage if left alone. I think she was right about this. On returning from a few days away I learned of her serious illness and called at her home late that night. The doctor came downstairs as I entered, a good doctor whom I knew well. He said that the patient would not live through the night. A quiet ministry brought her a sense of peace and the desire to sleep. I left the house knowing that two neighbours were staying through the night. The next day the sick woman got up and she outlived her husband by several years. Her selfless prayer was answered.

We ought always to ask for healing and be trustful when the answer (especially in old age) is a quiet passing into the life beyond. Jesus in His healing work could have had no thought of being disobedient to His Father's will. The recovery of the sick was a "sign" of the kingdom's power, and the imperfections and the disease that limited human life were part of the kingdom of evil that He came to destroy.

When the president of the synagogue criticised Jesus for healing the crippled woman on the Sabbath, our Lord replied, ". . . this woman, a daughter of Abraham, who has been kept prisoner by Satan for eighteen long years: was it wrong for her to be freed from her bonds on the Sabbath?" (Luke 13: 16). Satan had bound her—not God! God releases. It is a sign of the kingdom.

* * * *

Another source of misunderstanding is our failure to distinguish between suffering that is freely accepted and that which is imposed upon us and over which we have no control. There are some hardships that we need not accept but choose to do so, and some over which we have no choice. Paul speaks of his sufferings for the sake of the Gospel. He writes to the church at Corinth: "Five times the Jews have given me the thirty-nine strokes; three times I have been beaten with rods; once I was stoned; three times I have been shipwrecked, and for twenty-four hours I was adrift on the open sea" (2 Cor. II: 24-25). He goes on to tell of dangers on land and sea, from foreigners and his own countrymen, from hunger and cold. Hardships freely chosen in his love for the Gospel.

History is full of such experiences in men and women who would deny any pretence of sainthood yet have stood firm in the faith. Some have counted such suffering a joy, as Grenfell of Labrador did when he told an audience not to be sorry for him, for he was enjoying every minute of his work. It is a mistaken idea that pain or some deprivation always brings enrichment of character and is therefore God-sent for that purpose. The truth is that such limitation may well bring bitterness and resentment. Admittedly there are those great souls who are enriched by suffering, and when a man has some fearful handicap or is in constant pain yet has the spirit to rise above it, we can thank God for that. There is certainly a "Christian" attitude to such misfortune but it is no answer to make God the author of it.

It may well be God's will that the Albert Schweitzers and the Pauls of this world should forgo so much to serve their Lord, but this is a choice they freely make. Jesus made such a choice. Of course there was the risk that the world would reject Him. It did! A man may give his life in saving a child from a blazing building and it is surely God's will that he should have both the courage and the compassion to make the rescue attempt, but this does not mean that it is God's planned will that he should lose his own life in so doing. I will not believe that the Father, as Jesus revealed Him, would bring a child into this world and then will that the little life should be taken in a few months by leukaemia or meningitis. Such a belief cannot be reconciled with the picture that Jesus gave of a loving Father to whom we are urged to turn in need. It is a dishonest piety that says it can be.

Jesus did not argue about the origin of sickness. When the disciples asked Him why a man was born blind and whether he or his parents were the sinners, Jesus made it plain that it was not the sins of either. God's purpose could be seen not in the man's blindness but in his healing. Whatever "stops" there may be in your mind about it, Jesus treated disease as something alien to the perfect will of God. There is no conflict between the Father's loving purpose and the healing acts of His Son. Far better to believe that the Father wills our wholeness in spite of the hindrance to that will engineered by human folly or ignorance.

"I have come that men may have life, and have it in all its fullness" (John 10: 10). That is the word of our Lord and part of the mission committed to His disciples and to His Church. The power to make that mission possible is the promise that goes with it. It is so plain when the scriptures are opened up by Him who walks our Emmaus roads with us and, by the grace of God, stays with us to the point where we recognise Him and understand why our hearts have burned within us.

4

STILL ON THE EMMAUS ROAD

WE STAY WITH CLEOPAS and his friend as they make their way home with the stranger who has overtaken them. Moments when our hearts burn within us because of that same Companion are not uncommon in the work of Christian healing. So many have told me that they have never felt His nearness so surely as in a moment of healing prayer.

Like the two disciples, we may invite our Lord into our home and situation, only to discover that He has been with us all the time. It is then, in glad recognition, that we can share our certainties. Perhaps there is no better way of serving our fellows—or our Lord.

Nothing can so convince us of His healing power as the fact of experience. True, this may not overcome all our doubts or solve every problem, but at least we listen to a man who says with conviction, "Whereas I was blind, now I see." A woman sought the healing of Christ for double vision. This was a distressing condition that had not responded to treatment. The Lord healed her. This was not all, for she is able to share this with others, many of whom knew of her trouble and are in no doubt about her healing.

The Christ of history becomes the Christ of every day. His birth in Bethlehem proves to be, not just an intrusion into the human story, but an abiding. What can better convince us of the healing Lord than to see

Him in action and to meet those who have been blessed by His touch? This is illustrated by the story that follows.

I had just received a woman who was very distressed and unwell, and was talking to her in the vestry when we heard someone crying in the waiting-room. Another woman had arrived with an arm "locked" at the elbow and quite unable to move it. She came straight from the doctor's surgery and had been told to report to the hospital the next day. As the two women knew each other well, I took her into the vestry and prayed with her as the first visitor watched. The arm moved immediately and without pain and caused no further trouble. The first woman witnessed the power of Christ in her friend and feels sure that it contributed to her own healing.

Perhaps her own words will best tell her story. "I was ill with high blood-pressure and my doctor told me I must take life quietly. As I was a widow with the responsibility of a home and a rather worrying job to hold down, this advice was the last straw. I became depressed and on the edge of a nervous breakdown. Much of my time was spent in tears, full of fear and running away from people. After my first ministry I felt undergirded by prayer and after the third ministry I was back at work. Walking through the factory accompanied by a colleague—for I was still too fearful to walk alone—I suddenly felt my anxieties fall from me. I was free! Completely healed and with a deep joy that opened up a new life for me."

She became a dedicated member of the Prayer Fellowship and brought many to discover for themselves the power of her Lord. Resentments vanished and her outlook was transformed. I have known her for many years since then and, although she says that this is the greatest blessing she has ever known, she did not accept it selfishly. She lives a life of compassionate help to others and is one of the most encouraging people I know.

This is the challenge that comes to us all. To make known to others what God has done for us is not always easy, but it is rewarding if we have courage enough. When I first gathered a group around me to study this healing work I was still hesitant and uncertain. There were times when it would have been easy to give up and "go back home" as Cleopas intended to do. The day came when I was challenged in a way that made a choice urgent.

Walking from the Manse one morning to post a letter, I met a woman whom I knew slightly—I had not been long in that place—and she was on that disappointing road of despair. As I stepped by her side she opened her heart and told me her story. In her early thirties, the mother of two small children, she had undergone treatment for arthritis for two or three years. She had no complaints about her treatment, for everything medically possible had been done for her, but had now been told that nothing further could be done. She walked badly and was in constant pain and I think I have never seen anyone of her age so badly afflicted. Her head would not move separately from her body, for there was no movement in her neck, little strength in her right arm and less in the hand. Both hands were misshapen and every joint in arms and legs was affected.

And here was the challenge! If God really wanted me in this work maybe He was bringing me to the point of decision. It was like jumping off the deep end before I could swim! One thing I knew, it *was* a challenge, and if I did not accept it I should regret it all my life. I spoke to her of a Lord who heals today as He did in that Galilean ministry and she eagerly agreed to come to the Manse where my wife and I would seek God's help in prayer with her. The appointment was for the following day and I confess to being able to sleep very little that night. I need not have been so fearful, for the Lord was very near as I laid hands upon her in prayer. All three of us brought to that moment the preparation of our prayers and all the faith we could muster.

Within a few minutes of prayer her neck moved without pain although the grating noise unnerved us. Strength came again to arm and hand and she gripped quite firmly. We gave thanks to God and agreed that ministries should be continued each week, and this brought such improvement that she was soon able to work full-time—a very real need at that period. She was able to open the lock on the Manse door and open a tin of salmon when she got home, something she had not been able to manage for a long time. She reminded me, some thirteen years later, that soon after her healing she took up ballroom dancing and won a bronze medal. Her road of disappointed hopes became a road of new beginning.

Even on Emmaus roads of our experience, familiar roads on which the world never looks for His appearing, the Christian journey proves an adventure. How can it be otherwise when the Stranger who overtakes us on the way is the risen Lord whose love is big enough to redeem the world and personal enough to come in as a guest to the place where we live?

I wonder how that story in Luke's gospel would have

ended had they not invited Him to stay with them. He did not force His company on them. He never does! But they invited Him in and urged Him to stay overnight; and once inside their home, sharing their hospitality, He seemed less of a stranger. Some familiar gesture as He broke bread brought them to the moment of recognition and they had no doubt of His identity. Whatever we may make of that story, the carefully recorded details and the subsequent action of the disciples point to a genuine account. They would look with new insight on the things He said to them, an insight that added significance to words that had thrilled them as He spoke.

I suspect that we have walked many miles of our Emmaus roads without recognising Him and He must marvel at our dullness of mind. We walk with Him in casual companionship but do not invite Him into our homes where intimate fellowship can open our eyes to know Him for what He is. He has every right to be invited in. When we are ill we call the doctor. Every thinking man is thankful for the skills and discoveries of medical science. Where we fail in Christian understanding is that we do not always invite the Lord into the situation. We talk of His constant nearness but do not always act upon the truth of it.

I wonder what He thinks of our faith in Him when we do not even turn to Him for help until the doctor gives up! Such "last-resort" prayers are so often fearful and anxious that they are negative. It is the prayer of faith that fills us with His great spirit of healing power. Ask the Christ into your home, into the very heart of every situation, for He will share sorrows and joys and meet so many needs. To know His touch upon you and your loved ones in healing is to recognise the Christ who has already journeyed by your side. The unnoticed Christ is never absent but so often unacknowledged.

* * * *

Perhaps it is needful to put some emphasis on the truth that all healing comes from God. At best we can but make conditions right so that His healing can take place. To treat the Church's ministry of healing as divorced from medical care is to deny the Creator's part in every honest method that brings health to His people. We no longer fear some of the diseases that once brought panic to the whole community and we gladly acknowledge His encouragement and delight in every discovery that heals and blesses us.

There was a period when the Church and medicine parted company and the Church was much to blame. The scientific aspect of healing, crude enough in the beginning, moved on its way independently of some theological thinking that was not alive to the need for new knowledge and was hostile to any challenge to its authority. True, such scientific research moved on via a good many errors, but thank God it moved on. There is no real conflict between the two disciplines of religion and medicine, for both seek the truth and in whichever realm it is discovered the truth belongs to God. Had you asked Cleopas and his companion the truth of those happenings they had just witnessed, they would have said that Jesus was dead and buried. They would have been wrong! He was alive, and when they knew it despair was banished.

Doctor and minister are partners in the ministry that makes men whole. This is not always acknowledged but truth does not need to be acknowledged to be the truth. You can insist that the world is flat if you wish to, but no amount of insistence will make it so. Many claim that the Christian faith has nothing to do with healing in modern days although it did in the early centuries. Such scepticism may sound convincing enough but it need not be right in its denials. It is nearer the truth to say that the Church is looking with new faith, or at least with a new attitude, to the command of its Lord to heal the sick as well as to preach the gospel. This is coupled with a richer awareness of the power that flows in prayerful obedience. Where we are hesitant about the validity of Christ's promises, we should look again at the most unlikely promise of all as He assured His disciples that He would rise again. That promise was seen to be fulfilled on the Emmaus road. If *that* promise can be kept—and we are ready to believe it was—then surely the promised power to heal the sick is within the bounds of possibility.

See the immediate reaction as Cleopas and the other disciple recognised the Lord who had been crucified. Dreams that they had tried to forget filled their thoughts again, and the willing discipleship they had once been prepared to give claimed a new vigour. Hopes that had died on a hill outside Jerusalem were alive with new possibilities. Instead of going home they went straight back to adventure again. The other disciples must be told the news and so they go back along the old road with a new sense of power and hope that could not be contained.

There are moments when we too are led to such understanding and we know that the active, risen Lord is alive and with us. So we see roads that once were disappointing light up with new purpose. This ministry of healing is essentially practical. Theories abound, but when we feel His hand upon us or upon another with a power that cannot be denied, then we cannot but be challenged to adventure.

It happened like that to a minister friend of mine who hurt his back in a fall from a tree. Osteo-arthritis developed in the damaged spine and he was under frequent medical care and in hospital for periods of weeks each year for traction. He used a walking stick and was nearly always in pain. He hesitated for a long time, but eventually came across the city for a ministry of the laying-on-of-hands. He knew a healing far beyond the physical, for it resulted in his beginning a new and exciting ministry of healing in his own church. He puts his thoughts in a letter sent to me some years later and speaks for his wife as well as for himself.

"A great deal of our happiness and enrichment is due to you and we shall never forget your love and kindness in ministering to Mary and myself, and in being the instrument by which God led me to the healing work that widened and deepened my ministry in a way I still find hard to believe. . . ."

Many can thank God for experiences that send us back to tasks we were tempted to give up. Maybe to the place where we knew disappointment or to a work that proves more fruitful than we can dream of. Bible stories are frustratingly fragmentary and we can only assume that Cleopas and the other disciple completed the transition from discipleship to apostleship, from learner to teacher. It is reasonable to assume that they went back into the adventures of the New Testament Church and discovered, as their colleagues did, that, however deep their own convictions, it is not an easy thing to convince a sceptical world.

Great movements born of the Spirit that have left indelible marks on the Church's life have been pioneered against the odds of ridicule and unbelief. The Church's healing ministry, with all the evidence of growth, is still a pioneer movement to which we need to bring a sense of urgency and an adventurous spirit. There is undoubted value in shared experience where we discover God's strange arithmetic in which it is clear that two people working together are far more effective than the same two working in isolation. This work takes you right into the heart of things, for it is the most practical experience of prayer with which we may bless our fellows and glorify our Lord.

The world is waiting for the Christian Church to claim—and proclaim—its assurance of a Lord who keeps His word, who walks with us on every road. I have seen it happen too often to doubt its truth, that Christian men and women, in fellowship with their Lord, who care enough and will undertake the disciplines of prayer, will discover the gift of healing grace.

The healing and reconciling Christ stands in the midst of a praying people.

5

THE DAMASCUS ROAD

FOR SAUL, THIS WAS A ROAD of experience and change that he was destined never to forget, for on this road he came face to face with his Lord. It was not of his own seeking. Indeed he was resisting any thought of change and kicking against the goad. Most of us know this experience of resisting the Spirit's promptings, and wasted years can speak of our folly. You would not have convinced Saul that he did not meet with Christ that day. He never seemed to grow tired of telling the story.

Paul, as he was afterwards called, lived nearer to the time of the events recorded in the Gospel, but, like us, he never met Jesus during His earthly life. True, he had heard much of His work, enough to be biassed against a village carpenter who gathered a few uneducated fishermen around Him and made preposterous claims of relationship with God. He determined to crush this heretical movement once and for all, and had watched while Stephen was stoned to death. It is so easy to kick against the goad and resist acceptance of something we do not want to believe.

My own road to the healing ministry began with a mild feeling of opposition to it. I accepted the records of the healings by Jesus and His disciples but felt that they belonged to the New Testament era. It was therefore easy to dismiss claims of healing power as some psychological effect upon credulous people. I say this to my shame, for my own little son, at three years old, was given a few hours to live but, surrounded by the prayers of many Christian friends, was restored to health.

Be thankful for Damascus roads that can shock us into the truth by a confrontation with our Lord that we can no longer deny. Paul was blinded by prejudice and a fanaticism that can keep us strangely blinkered to the truth, and lead us to the fear that persecutes our opponents. Such was his mood as he set out for Damascus. A momentous confrontation with Jesus brought physical—or psychological—blindness from which he was later healed as Ananias laid hands in prayer upon him. With sight restored he began a life's work in which he never doubted that the Christ he met on the Damascus road was with him on every road.

It is not easily understood that a man can be "called" by God to a work that he would not otherwise do, or indeed be able to do, yet it is hardly credible that Paul's loyalty could be sustained through the years if its inspiration was nothing but a personal whim. He never doubted his divine call and insisted that it was not a vision or a foolish dream that set him on his mission. It was a meeting with his Lord. We may doubt human wisdom in responding to a call which denies a man much that the world can offer, yet will not let him forget the moment of assurance that set him on his way. Some things cannot be explained in human terms but we have no right to deny the validity of such an encounter because we have not experienced it. Thank God for the Damascus roads on which our Lord reveals Himself and makes demands that we cannot resist.

This same truth is discovered in the ministry of healing. The call to it can be real enough and we are challenged to make up our minds about it. It knocks at the door of our conscience and demands to be noticed as the deep needs of our fellows cry out for help. No man is whole if, like the curate's egg, he is good only in parts. The wholeness that Christ gives is the concern of every man. We ought to make a judgement on it if we are to be honest, for we owe it to our fellows and our Lord to make up our minds.

The need is so obvious. There is hardly a family without some deep problem of illness or difficulty and we dare not miss the opportunities God gives us to bring human need and divine help together. To read the right kind of literature about the Church's healing work and to examine the evidence is, at least, to have some knowledge of the facts. We shall make few discoveries in any field if our minds are closed and our knowledge is deliberately or carelessly limited. Paul's experience on that road of change led him to the truth of the very things he had once denied. He now believed what he would not have accepted in the flaming days of "threatenings and slaughter". This was not merely academic belief, but truth he was ready to wager his life on.

He had sources of information more personal than ours can be and he undoubtedly learned much from those who were eye-witnesses, but he affirmed his conviction that his new-found faith did not come from hearsay but from the Lord Himself. In a less dramatic way, but none the less real, we may still be aware of the Spirit's leading. I have been grateful for it many times when ministering to someone with a problem that human wisdom (mine, anyway!) could never solve. God may well have a word for us as we wait upon Him in prayer; and reference to the story already told of the woman who was locked with arthritis, illustrates this point. Ministries had brought such relief and freedom of movement, but one day the prompting seemed so clear that I said to her, "If stiffness and pain should return in spite of your steady progress, do not despair. The Lord has healed you so far and can surely complete what He has begun." I was grateful for that prompting, for within a few days this very thing happened. After a morning service one Sunday she told me of a reversal of the improvement in her condition, and a return of pain. True, this was much less severe than formerly, and a prayer in which two of my deacons shared brought immediate relief which continued.

An overworked minister in a London parish who gave himself so consistently was asked by a friend how he kept going. He replied simply, "We get help!" So indeed we do. However much this may be doubted in some minds the prompting of the Holy Spirit is a reality without which so much of our Christian work could not be done. Paul travelled endless miles after that confrontation with Christ in the knowledge that he was never alone. A Divine call brings with it a promise of a Divine Companion.

Let your conclusions be reached fairly as you consider the validity of the Church's healing work. Turn it down if you will—but not without an honest judgement, for it is too easy to prejudge an issue and get the wrong answer if we are not ready to bring to it the humility of a learner. Without that humility you will miss the way. To sit on the fence of half-hearted commitment is to miss the challenges of a work that is both exacting and exciting. If it is true that the Christ is with us on modern roads, compassionately concerned about our situations and seeking to heal the wounds that limit human life, then we ought to proclaim it from the housetops! Why be ashamed that we give our loyalty, not to some vague figure of history, but to a risen and active Lord? See the profound simplicity of this almost unbelievable story of a Christ who not only confronted Saul on his prejudiced and unbelieving road but also knew where he lived! Ananias was sent to the street called Straight to heal the bewildered blindness of that zealous man. HE knows where *you* live! Knows your deepest needs. We cannot put too much stress on the truth of the personal concern of our Lord for His people, for this adds a sense of reality to our prayers.

I suspect that many of us have known moments when we have been prompted to some action that seemed to be contrary to common sense. I had already begun an afternoon round of visiting when I felt a strong sense of urgency to visit someone I had heard about but never met. (The story of her subsequent healing is found in Chapter 8.) One of my members had told me of her daughter who was near breakdown and was under psychiatric treatment. The prompting was clear that I should change my intended programme that day and go to see her instead. I did not even know where she lived, so went to the mother's home to find out. Finding no one at home I enquired of a neighbour who gave me the name of the village but did not know the address. It would have been easy to await more information but the prompting was so strong that I set out for the village, some miles away, and eventually found the house I sought. The young married woman was home with her husband and was deeply distressed. A ministry calmed and assured her and led to her healing. We were in no doubt of the leading of the Spirit that day, for she and her husband are now committed to the Christian way.

What a gospel this is to proclaim to the world, that the Christ steps from the remoteness of New Testament days and meets you where you are and knows where you live! To believe that our Lord cares so much is to pay gladly the cost of the disciplines that compassion and faith lay upon us.

More than I can number among my colleagues have longed to have a more positive part in this ministry of healing but have never taken that first step in faith—a step that would soon convince them of its worth. They feel the impelling power of it but cannot bring themselves to full commitment. This is not said in judgement, for we live in an age where the climate of faith demands intellectual assurance. There should be a reason for the faith that is in us, for ours is a revealed religion which makes demands on more than the heart; and, while proof is a legitimate demand in some spheres, it may not be in others.

There are some areas of experience where there is not, and can never be, scientific proof. Being in love is a real enough experience, but you cannot measure and weigh it in the laboratory. The chemist may make a chemical analysis of a tear-drop but he cannot even begin to describe the anguish that made the tear run down your cheek. Words are not adequate to describe what it means to feel the power of the healing Christ fill your whole being. The blind man healed by Jesus was asked how it was done. He didn't know, but one thing he did know was that whereas once he was blind, now he could see. He could offer no explanation that would satisfy the mind, but that did not matter so much as the fact that he was no longer in a world of darkness.

No man can be obedient to the command to lay hands upon the sick in the name of Jesus unless he has faith enough to take that step. He will never be so used if he insists on a certainty that cannot come until he puts faith to a confident test. What he needs is faith in Christ, not in himself, for healing comes not by our own power but by His.

Commonsense convinced Saul that a village carpenter's son could not be the Messiah—until he met Him on the Damascus road. No amount of argument would have led him to the truth. We ought not to demand of this ministry more "proof" and more guarantee of success than we ask of God in any other call He may give us. To kick against the goad may seem to be human wisdom, but it never leads to the experiences that can come when a man leans the full weight of his faith upon God. We cannot do alone what can be done only in partnership with our Lord and we dare not put a limit on what God can do through us. *We* cannot fill a soul with the Holy Spirit, nor can we bring healing to another in our own strength.

History makes it plain that the kingdom is brought nearer by partnership, by the mad, foolish dreams of men and women who believe in what they and God can do together. They have dared to bet their lives on a hope that seemed foolish in human eyes—even as the cross has been seen as foolishness and a stumbling block. What hopes had Carey or Livingstone, Wesley or Paul to achieve their dreams, save hope in their Lord? The impossible becomes possible in Christ as we are prepared to be fools for His sake. The possibility of failure makes us fear that we shall look foolish, so we hesitate and kick against that which goads us to full obedience. I confess that this was a formidable hurdle to me and I was fearful of being left alone in the valley of challenge while Christ was away on some Mount of Transfiguration.

The Damascus road is a road of change and of challenge and assurance of the promised presence of Christ, but not an insurance against human failure. Risk is inherent in adventure and this is a road of adventure where prejudice is changed to faith. It is not *we* who heal, but Christ. To blame ourselves for failure and demand impossible guarantees is perhaps a back-handed way of crediting ourselves with success, and we have no right to do that. Our Lord asks of us the best that we can do and the best that we can be, so that in partnership He can use us to do His will. Remember that He has always used imperfect people, for He has never had any other kind to use.

There are no finer moments in any man's life than those when, knowing his own inadequacy, he leans in happy trust upon his Lord. What is needed of us in this work is a compassion that cares enough, a faith that will be obedient, a trust that leaves the results in Divine hands and the humility to be unafraid of what the world will call failure. Some have suggested that to come in hope of healing and be left unhealed is to risk losing the faith we have. I have never found this to be so. To receive such a ministry, even when physical healing is delayed or does not come, is an enriching experience. Healing does come in such moments, too often for us to doubt the power that Christ promised.

Here is one sphere in which you cannot make an

honest judgement unless you have sought in faith to know His touch. In every realm some prayers appear to remain unanswered but we do not stop praying. A sick man does not refuse his doctor's help because some of his patients have not recovered. I can only state the simple fact that in years of this ministry the Christ has never been more real to me than when I have sought His help for my people in their dire need. I believe it to be true that, of all the scores of people I have been privileged to minister to, not one, so far as I know, has lost faith in God. So many have had their faith brought to a new level of wonder and delight as they have known the peace of His touch upon them. We must remember that if there are failures there are also successes —though neither word, in my view, is the right one to use.

There are obvious results for which we can be grateful, when, for example, locked limbs are freed or pain is banished or relieved. A woman came to my Vestry Hour one Saturday morning in a distressed and unhappy state. She had trouble with a painful arm which would not move beyond a limited degree and which had not responded to some six months of treatment. She had been brought by a friend; we prayed together and her arm became free to move without pain. She went straight from the ministry to a city some eight miles away for an afternoon's shopping and had no further trouble.

Such immediate help can come to other conditions too. A young woman under training for a medical career had such an illness which made study impossible. Out-patient treatment in a psychiatric hospital led to a suggested stay as an in-patient. Her father brought her to the Vestry Hour and she was healed that night. As a discharged patient she went for occasional check-ups but had no further trouble.

Thank God for modern Damascus roads on which we may meet our risen Lord; for His goading that will not let us rest and sends us on uncharted journeys! Thank God for the faithful ministries of some modern Ananias by which our vision is cleared and our way made plain! Grateful too, for those deep experiences which assure us of the unchanging Christ and make it inevitable that we should not be “disobedient to the heavenly vision”.

6

THE ROAD TO THE TEMPLE

NEW TESTAMENT ROADS on which men and women confronted the Healing Christ have their counterparts on the roads we know. Where more should He be found than on the road that leads to (and from) the Christian Church? A deep experience of worship brings an awareness of our Lord and sets the right climate for us to grow in. In this chapter we recall the story in the Acts of the Apostles where Peter and John walked together to the temple. Their minds were set on giving thanks to God and must have been filled with the amazing truth of Easter Day and the period which followed in which the risen Lord was so wonderfully near.

Those forty days between the resurrection and the ascension were full of meaning. The disciples never knew when to expect Jesus, for He appeared in many differing circumstances. On the sea-shore; when they were hiding in fear in a locked room; on the Emmaus road and elsewhere. Time and distance were no hindrance to Him, for He was no longer limited by a human body. He came to them wherever they were and whatever they were doing and they learned that an invisible Lord was with them always. He was the same Lord whom they had loved and served and as real as when He was alive among them. This was made clear in those forty days as the living Lord led them through doubt and uncertainty to a life-changing assurance.

Not just Peter and John on the way to the temple, but Peter and John *and* their Lord. Let the account come alive as we read it and discover that meaningful worship puts us on our road to the temple by the side of the same Lord. We may have little silver or gold, but what we do have we may give in the name of Peter's Lord and ours. "One day at three in the afternoon, the hour of prayer, Peter and John were on their way up to the temple. Now a man who had been a cripple from birth used to be carried there and laid every day by the gate of the temple called 'Beautiful Gate', to beg from people as they went in. When he saw Peter and John on their way into the temple he asked for charity. But Peter fixed his eyes on him, as John did also, and said, 'Look at us.' Expecting a gift from them, the man was all attention. And Peter said, 'I have no silver or gold; but what I have I give you: in the name of Jesus Christ of Nazareth, walk.' Then he grasped him by the right hand and pulled him up; and at once his feet and ankles grew strong; he sprang up, stood on his feet, and started to walk." (Acts 3: 1-8).

"What I have I give you." It would have been easier to toss a careless coin into the beggar's bowl, but how small a gift it would have been compared with what the disciples offered in the name of their Lord. It is a sad commentary on our times that we can offer silver and gold more easily than we can offer the quiet assurance of the uplifting and healing power of the Church's Lord. We have not always encouraged faith in the Healing Christ, though there are signs that this gift to the Church is more fully recognised than once it was.

Maybe God is calling us again to "Give what we have"—and maybe we are learning afresh that we have this partnership in His continuing work of bringing wholeness and healing to His people. The gift is ours to give did we but know it.

To acknowledge this ministry as an integral part of the Church's life is no affront to orthodox medicine. Gladly accepting what is done for us, we still see the truth that the Church has something more to give, for it has the promised power of the Lord. In the Christian faith there is an added "something" that can come from no other source.

History makes it clear that when the mainstream of the Christian Church neglects or ignores some aspect of its full mission, God raises up some faithful soul to bring it back into focus. I realise that it may be an over-simplification, but this is basically what happened at the Reformation. Since then we have seen how neglected aspects of the Gospel are taken up by those who find the Church is not supple enough to change its pattern. They have been led to forsake the main body of Christian thought in order to be obedient to what they feel to be a vital truth. The resultant sect will then emphasise what was neglected, and sometimes it can be an over-emphasis so that they, in turn, neglect parts of the Gospel's contents which others feel to be important.

Our Lord's command to His disciples to preach and heal is so clearly a part of His continuing work that it should be acknowledged as such, and recognised as part of the life and work of every Christian community. We owe it to our Lord and to our fellows to be aware of its challenge. It in no way detracts from the worth of the many other aspects of Christian witness and ministry.

Jesus came with that wide, all-embracing purpose that included this life and the life hereafter, and we must put no false limits on His mission. His work on earth shows a constant concern for human need, and it would seem proper to seek this healing gift *within* the Church and not as something separate from it and almost in opposition to it.

Evidence of the effectiveness of this ministry is too plentiful for us to deny its place in our thinking and gives us no right to ignore it. Who will blame the world for condemning a half-hearted faith and finding it unattractive? Those whose faith is newly awakened will not be thrilled to walk that road to the "temple" with Christians who have ceased to find any joy in their faith and who do not expect the promises of their Lord to be fulfilled. The Church is too often on the defensive when it should be advancing to challenge the world, but first it must challenge its own faith and attitudes and demonstrate in its own life that it really believes in a Christ who can heal the deep wounds of mankind.

The world will not listen forever to the reiteration of an account of a Christ who once lived, but may well respond to a faith in a living Christ who is still active in human affairs. On the road to the "temple" men and women expect to find evidence of the reality of the Lord we worship. This is the challenge the world makes to the modern Church—that we are responsive not to some vague principle, but to a Lord whom we *know* and with whom we walk with confidence and trust. "What I have I give you," said Peter, and no man can give something he hasn't got. If the Church's larder is empty, how can men be given bread? We are sometimes like the man in the parable who had an unexpected visitor and had to confess that he had nothing to set before him. God forgive us if we have not the bread we claimed was ours when men and women, hungry and in need, call on us on their journey.

The road that leads us to worship also leads to healing and wholeness, for it brings us face to face with Him who promised to fill life with a new fullness. The Sacraments, the preaching of the Word and the act of prayer, witness together to the power of the Church's Lord. They are not separate acts. They belong together. To worship is to be in the very climate of growth and healing and renewal. We often hear of the experience in the baptism of a sick child in which healing has come in a way that is inexplicable to medical knowledge. A young woman came for healing prayer for a painful condition that would not respond to treatment. There was no apparent result of that ministry, but a few days later healing came as she attended a service of Holy Communion in my church, led by a minister who knew nothing of her condition or need. The healing of Christ can come within the context of worship and an atmosphere of prayer. The trouble is that we are not expectant enough—and certainly we do not always give our Lord thanks or even the credit when healing comes.

Some seek the healing of God in prayer and when they receive it they find some other reason to explain their healing. Quite late one Saturday evening I was asked to visit a woman who was very ill with pain in the head that could not be relieved. She had not been able to sleep for several nights and was obviously very tired. Her sister was preparing soup when I arrived. I ministered to the sick woman with prayer and laid my hands on her feverish head. She relaxed and was on the point of sleep as I left the room. I suggested to her sister that she should not be wakened if she was asleep when the soup was prepared, as her great need was for rest. I called at the home before Morning Service next day. The sister came to the door and said brightly, "She had a wonderful night's sleep. I gave her three aspirins after you had gone, and they worked!"

We must not let the fear of being credulous rob us of our gratitude, nor must we ask so much of our Lord and then doubt His part in answered prayer. Believe in the presence of Jesus as you worship Him and discover the wonder of fellowship in which healing power is part of the very atmosphere. Worship has this therapeutic quality, for it brings us close to that kingdom of wholeness Jesus declared to have come. That kingdom is more than the hope of eternal life—it is the experience of those who receive Him. Remember when He sent out the seventy-two on that mission of preaching and healing? "When you come into a town and they make you welcome, eat the food provided for you; heal the sick there, and say, 'The kingdom of God has come close to you.' When you enter a town and they do not make you welcome, go out into its streets and say, 'The very dust of your town that clings to our feet we wipe off to your shame. Only take note of this: the kingdom of God has come close'" (Luke 10: 8-11).

In worship, that kingdom can be strangely near. In thanksgiving or praise, in music or prayer, in the definite act of asking, in adoration or confession —whatever we offer to the Father in worship can bring us to a moment when the kingdom can be ours. True, there are those who tell us that worship is unimportant and that God does not need it. All He needs is practical service to our fellows, they tell us, and quote the words of Jesus to prove it. "I tell you this: anything you did for one of my brothers here, however humble, you did for me" (Matt. 25: 40). Experience soon shows that it is a mistake to divide the two aspects of worship and service, for both are vital needs. We cannot give out any kind of enabling power to others unless we keep our own spiritual batteries charged. Jesus knew that need Himself, and if He needed fellowship with God in worship and prayer, what fools we are to think that we can do without it! There is nowhere where you can so surely find strength and power and inspiration to re-make your own life and serve your fellows as in the act of worship. You may be sure that one road on which you may hope to find the Healing Christ is on the road to the temple.

True, your own attitude is important, for you would hardly find such strength and inspiration if you deny the power of the Lord you worship. Many are doubtful and some are even hostile. Jesus found hostility as He met someone in deep need in the synagogue. "There was a woman there possessed by a spirit that had crippled her for eighteen years. She was bent double . . ." (Luke 13: 10-11). Jesus healed her, but the president of the synagogue, the very man who should have been leading his people to their God, could not see the Divine will in what was happening before his eyes. Sure, there are those who deny the power of Jesus to release and set free those who are bound by sickness. They deny the Church's part in this commission, but this does not mean that the Christ is not at work within the Church and within those who are ready to take Him at His word. He is limited only by our lack of faith—limited within His own territory, the Christian fellowship, just as He was limited by such lack of faith in His own town at Nazareth.

On holiday I met a woman who had not been able to stand upright for some years. She was in her eighties and arthritis in neck and spine locked her in a forward leaning position. Our meeting was arranged by a mutual friend and we came to that ministry with prayerful preparation. I remember how we thanked God together as, under prayer and the laying-on-of-hands, she was able to stand erect. She stood upright with her head pressed against the wall behind her, saying, "I haven't seen the ceiling for eight years." The Lord who healed when He was upon this earth still does!

It was on their way to church that Peter and John met the challenge of a man crippled from birth. Others could have supplied part of his need, for he might go hungry without their help. Much human need is met by the society in which we live. Thank God for the help the world can give—and so often does! Mankind would be poor indeed without the generosity of the many who own no Christian allegiance. The beggar at the temple gate relied on common humanity. He was indebted to those who carried him to his place each day and to those who gave him money as they passed by. Where generosity is born of compassion, that ministry is blessed by God, whether it be religious or secular help. It is a common Christian duty to be aware of such agencies, for through them Christian and non-Christian alike can share in service to their fellows. Practical helpfulness is possible from us all.

It is obvious enough that medicine and psychiatry should be left to those who are trained in such disciplines and are equipped to practise them. But do not lose sight of the ministries that are possible because a man has faith in God. The Church has a commission to serve—a call that it shares with others; but it also has gifts of healing in its Lord that may not be recognised elsewhere. It is our business to know something of that commission within the Church's life. It is our business, too, to know far more than we do about prayer. For prayer not only adds a vitality to our service for others, but is the channel through which power flows from the very source of life itself. This is wonderfully revealed in Christian fellowship in a way that leaves its mark upon us. What we are makes its mark upon the community in which we live. There are some things that cannot be accomplished save in a partnership of faith in God and in our fellows. Prayer opens doors that might otherwise remain closed, and where should prayer be more firmly backed up by trust than within the fellowship that upbuilds the corporate life of its members and trusts in its divine Leader? There are many things better done in fellowship than in isolation. What we cannot hope to do alone *can* be done by God and us together. This is the truth we must proclaim from the housetops, for the world is waiting to hear it.

"What I have I give you." What God gives to us we can channel to others if we have faith and love enough. This truth may be hidden from the wise; it may be denied or ridiculed; it may seem foolish in the eyes of the world—but it is demonstrated every day if we have faith to believe it and courage enough to put it to the test. Two people spoke to me after a service of healing in which many received ministries. Both had intended to come forward for prayer but felt the healing of Christ as they prayed for others. They actually felt the warmth and vibration that often come with the laying-on-of-hands although there was no physical contact. In the act of worship, they knew healing.

The Church should gladly acknowledge the strength of fellowship in prayer. Discipline has its rightful place but will not thrill us as faith in a loving Lord will. On the road to the temple—in the fellowship of the Christian Church—we discover, not only our fellows' need, but also a Lord whose power to get a man on his feet again is undeniable. That we are privileged to channel healing grace to others is no cause for pride but for gratitude. Pride is born of self-sufficiency, whereas gratitude is born of a glad reliance on another. When that "other" is the Christ, there is no false humility but a glad acceptance of partnership.

Of the scores of men and women who passed by the beggar on their way to the temple, some may have tossed a coin into his outstretched hands. Peter and John had something more to give. Christ the healer—Peter the link between Divine aid and human need. A glad partnership indeed! In such co-operation the man of faith can reach out human hands in ways far beyond his own strength. "In the name of Jesus of Nazareth, walk!" What a stupid thing to say to a man who had been crippled all his life! Stupid it would be, if the command had been nothing more than human advice, but Peter grasped that outstretched hand with assurance and spoke with quiet authority. He had already learned much about his own limitations, as we have, but he also knew his Lord and had faith enough to be the link between the man's need and the One who could meet it.

This book would never have been written but for the belief that many such gaps can be bridged if we keep one hand in Christ's and reach out with the other to grasp the hand of those who need Him.

This is part of our challenge on the way to the temple. We do not need to be reminded of human need, for it is always with us. Some we might meet with silver and gold, but much is too deep to be healed by charity. We have the promise of power—and if we have eyes to see and ears to hear, we have evidence enough of answered prayer in lives changed and renewed and made whole. "What I have I give you." Christian fellowship within an imperfect Church is not the failure some would have us believe.

Never despise the road to the temple, for there you may find the strength of fellowship with your Lord and have spiritual batteries re-charged to give power for the journey. Give in gratitude. Ask in prayer. Serve your fellows. Not only with silver and gold and human advice—though these have their place—but with the calm assurance of a faith that can say with confidence, "In the name of Jesus of Nazareth, get on your feet, man!"

7

THE ROAD OF ASSURANCE

A MINISTER ONCE SAID to me, "If I could have just one of the experiences of healing prayer that you have had in your ministry, I should never doubt again." He *might*, you know! We may feel ashamed to admit it, but so often it is true that faith is a battle to keep doubts quiet. This need not be the conflict it suggests, for the real secret lies not so much in battle as in quiet surrender. Difficult enough when under stress or in painful and anxious moments, it is still true that the secret of healing grace is acceptance. Let us admit our constant need of fuel to feed the fires of faith. We need this road of assurance.

There is no need to be ashamed of stepping out along any road that encourages us in the belief that our most hopeful moments are the moments to trust. We see the value of prayer groups in this very thing, as we share experiences and encourage one another. There are aids to faith that we ought not to ignore. The re-reading of one of the New Testament healings can shed new light on a dark road. The Gospel has such convincing power. To share experiences with others to whom the Christ is real is to have our own faith lifted to loftier heights. The evidence that Christ has touched a life with wholeness may well be the assurance we need when we find ourselves prisoners of doubt.

It is also true that we may not have had such first-hand evidence, not for the moment anyway, and we have to rely on the trusted word of another. John the Baptist found this to be true when he was in prison and unable to see for himself what Jesus was doing. He sent his friends to make enquiry and bring him word. Who can blame John for wondering if he had been mistaken in thinking that his cousin was the Messiah?

The Baptist had come to the end of his own work of proclaiming a coming Lord and was in prison, soon to be murdered at the whim of a scheming woman. Could he have been wrong? It would be easy to think so as he remained a prisoner. If Jesus was Messiah would He not have called upon heavenly resources to set him free? Who better than the Baptist would have made a loyal follower? He had already shown a fine character in taking second place and gladly proclaiming Jesus as Israel's deliverer. No wonder doubts persisted as the days went by and he was still a prisoner.

It seems that John had freedom enough to keep in contact with his friends whom he had gathered as disciples around him. They kept him informed of the healing work of Jesus, but still he wondered if he had been mistaken. He sent his friends to ask Jesus outright. A widow's son had been raised from the dead, and crowds, awed by this great show of power, gave thanks to God and talked of a great prophet who had come amongst them. By such acts of compassion He demonstrated the caring love of God.

John was informed of all this, and calling two of his disciples, he sent them questioning to the Lord. Look at the narrative again as they sought out Jesus. "John the Baptist has sent us to you: he asks, 'Are you the one who is to come, or are we to expect some other?' There and then he cured many sufferers from diseases, plagues and evil spirits: and on many blind people he bestowed sight. Then he gave them his answer: 'Go,' he said, ' and tell John what you have seen and heard: how the blind recover their sight, the lame walk, the lepers are made clean, the deaf hear, the dead are raised to life, the poor are hearing the good news—and happy is the man who does not find me a stumbling block' " (Luke 7:19-23).

This is one of the many unfinished stories of the Bible. We do not know how John reacted to the disciples' report, for his death came without warning. But we can see how we need to rely on the witness of others. Most of us know such "messengers" whom we can trust to tell us the truth and who have witnessed in themselves or in others the power of Christ's healing. They come back to our imprisoning doubts and tell us the good news. Thank God for them; they help us on the road to assurance and carry us on some of its miles by their conviction.

What a variety of needs Jesus met in this short account! Everyone has something missing, for none is complete and whole. Our lives are broken and fragmentary so that all men need the wholeness Jesus came to bring. He deals with us one at a time. Note how personal His ministry is. Not indiscriminate healing or some mass ministration, but the personal touch. To see Him influencing broken lives is to be assured of the power still available in Him. What a joy to meet those who are so wonderfully sure of Him! One of the rewards of this ministry is to meet again those who were healed long since and have maintained their faith through the years. Like the blind man healed by Jesus, they do not know all the answers—but they know that they have been healed.

Meet, where you can, those who have known the impact of the Healing Christ and let them set your doubts at rest. If we are the "Johns" who make enquiry they can tell us what they have seen and heard and experienced for themselves. They set us again on the road to assurance. God knows, we need such reminders, for we have too many dull moments of uncertainty, and every signpost that points the way to renewed faith should be welcomed.

I remember one period when I was a little dispirited and a member of my prayer group said quietly, "If only one person is healed and brought close to our Lord in a whole year it is worth our meeting every week." I have always been grateful for those words. Thank God when such periods of dullness are short-lived and when the sunshine of assurance floods our path with light. It is easy to be wise after the event, but doubts that are real enough at the time and almost overwhelm us can be proved to be wrong.

Under some pressure from his wife a man whose arms were locked in a bent position came to my Vestry Hour. After a ministry his arms were still locked and I remember the sense of disappointment I felt as he left the vestry with the promise to come to my home the next day for further prayer. The following morning he walked, swinging his arms, and said that they were freely moving by the time he reached home the night before.

"Go and tell John what you see . . ."

Every agency that can turn a road of doubt into a highway of hope is to be welcomed. For some it may be a quiet waiting upon God that leads to the point where trust is restored. Maybe the word of another will set the blood racing with new hope, or the reading of a book will take us right into the heart of someone's deep experience. To read the Bible with fresh eyes can be a profound and moving experience that can bring us to a calm certainty that there is a promised power beyond our comprehension. However easy it is to get on to roads of doubt and mistrust, the Holy Spirit prompts and guides us to a glad faith again.

There will be times when we are on the rebellious road to Damascus or on the disappointing road to Emmaus. We shall often be on the Jericho road of human need and find that our store of oil and wine runs low, and even our compassion allows the world to hint that it would be wise to pass by on the other side before we are hurt and heart-broken by our inadequacy.

If we keep true to our calling we are seldom off that Jericho road where many come to the end of their hope of human help and turn to the Lord in desperation. In a former church we ran a series of special services. Many new houses had been built in the district and we made a point of publicity. Leaflets went into every home telling of the services arranged, assuring everyone of a warm welcome and outlining the activities and life of the church. Among many items the Prayer and Healing Fellowship and the Minister's Vestry Hour were mentioned.

The response was disappointing at the time, though we later proved that bread is never cast upon the waters in vain. A week or two after the leaflets were distributed a young mother of two children came with much hesitation to the Vestry Hour. Her distress was pitiful as she came in pale and trembling and full of fear. She broke down completely but eventually told her story.

That morning she had prepared an overdose of aspirin and had spent the day struggling against the temptation to take her own life. Following a compulsory move to a new flat she had known weeks of anxiety but had managed to keep it from her husband. They had moved from a small, low-rented house near to her husband's work and, confronted with greatly increased costs in rent and transport and the need to furnish the new home, she broke down under the strain of it all.

The church's leaflet was in her hand and she confessed that she had slept with it under her pillow and looked at it a dozen times a day. Now she had found courage to come. She became wonderfully calm as I laid my hands upon her in prayer and we shared her problems in the undoubted presence of our Lord. I think I have never been more sure of His touch. She was healed that night! Healed in spirit so that the burden was lifted and she was free to think calmly. I knew she would go back straight away to her husband, for whom she had so obvious an affection.

A visit to her home and family the next day and again within the week, a sharing with husband and wife together brought peace and hope to the situation. Problems were real enough but were calmly faced and worked out. The next week found husband and wife and children at the church asking that we might thank God together for the Lord who had brought such change to their home and saved that little family from tragedy.

Never keep God too small in your thinking so that, while you credit Him with power to create this vast universe, you do not see Him big enough to be compassionately concerned about human situations. He *is* big enough! He is concerned about us! This makes prayer not a vague calling for help from some unknown power, but an intimate sharing with our Father. Prayer that is as personal as that, brings us close to the kingdom which Jesus told His disciples to declare to be "already among" those to whom they ministered in His name.

From trusted friends who had been eyewitnesses to the healing work of Jesus, reassuring news came back to the Baptist in his prison house. Not a collection of stories told by others—which might have lost nothing in the telling, but something they had seen for themselves. Nothing less would have satisfied John. Miracles of healing were no proof of the Lord's Messiahship. We may approach the thought of Messiahship without too many preconceived ideas, but it was impossible for a Jew to do so. Maybe that is why Jesus added that final word to the enquiring John. "Happy is the man who does not find me a stumbling block"—a word we would do well to accept for ourselves.

The Jews had long thought of the Messiah as one who would come with power and in judgement. True, there were Old Testament prophecies which told of healing the sick and this part seems to have been fulfilled in Jesus, but He had not proclaimed His Messiahship with some great, unmistakable flourish. He was teaching in a way that left men free to make up their own minds whether or not to accept Him. In many ways He was not fulfilling Jewish expectation and even the disciples must have taken Him for a teacher or a prophet, sent by God—maybe—but it was a long road from that call by the seashore to Peter's great affirmation at Philippi. "Who do men say I am?" asked Jesus as they set out for the villages of Caesarea Philippi. "They answered,

'Some say John the Baptist, others Elijah, others one of the prophets.' 'And you,' he asked, 'who do you say I am?' Peter replied: 'You are the Messiah'" (Mark 8:27-29).

Belief in the power of Jesus can be hindered if we doubt His Messiahship. We may say of Jesus that you cannot ask too much of Him, for with Him all things are possible. You cannot say that of a prophet! You *can* say that about Jesus, but even so the questions tumble over one another waiting to be answered. Why are some not healed? Why was the Baptist left to die while Peter was rescued from prison? The word "Why" begins so many sentences and is the question that, more than others, leaves us dumb and without an answer. We stumble when we are not sure of Him and ask for "signs" to bolster up our belief. Then we are told that this is the wrong way round, that "Signs *follow* belief" and are the result of the prayer of faith. It is faith we need, and not proof as the world thinks of that word.

The road to assurance has its signposts for which we are grateful: personal experience which speaks so plainly; the experience of those whose word we can trust; the New Testament Word that tells of the healing Lord. These are signposts to the road of assurance on which we can step out with confidence as we walk with a Lord who put His trust in God.

I cannot prove to you that the Lord is so wonderfully near as I minister to those in dire need—and *you* cannot prove that He isn't! So we move inevitably to the realm of faith and thank God for moments when we find it to be assurance enough.

8

THE ROAD OF TODAY

FROM THE DUSTY LANES of Galilee in the first century to the motorways of the twentieth century is a long trek. Not a long time in years maybe, when we compare it with the centuries of recorded and unrecorded history, but still, humanly speaking, a long time. It is this period that concerns us as we think of healing that has its setting within the Christian faith. Not that healing is confined to the Christian conception of life, but we are thinking of that to which Jesus called the world's attention and to which He commissioned His disciples.

This chapter and many others could be filled with stories of men and women who have known healing in this ministry and who are convinced that the Christ still walks on the modern, familiar roads of today. The human journey lights up with new meaning when we discover Him and know His kingdom to be our inheritance.

There is a story told of a man who walked through a gentleman's estate as a short cut to the factory where he worked. The great park with its lakes and outbuildings, the fine old house itself, all came within his view each day, but he hardly noticed them. It was his common road of everyday—a short cut to his place of work. Then the estate owner died and left the whole of his property to the workman. See the difference! The road he once used every day and hardly noticed now took on a new significance. He owned it! It was his!

We have such an inheritance and when we realise that it really *is* ours, our common road is seen with new eyes. We look with the eyes of ownership on something the commonplace never offered before. Office or factory, home or market place or church take on a new dimension.

It never ceases to be a wonder to me that the commonplace can be so transformed. In an act of healing prayer—more than in anything I know—we can so wonderfully turn from the ordinary to the sublime; from life's anxieties, from work and conversation, from problems and doubts, and find our true inheritance in Divine companionship. More people than we might suppose find this to be true as many, without much former experience of Him, meet with the Lord of everyday.

One would imagine that this technological age would not be conducive to such discovery in spiritual things. It is so clearly an age of man's self-sufficiency and the thought comes easily to modern minds that we can do without God. What need is there to pray for daily bread when we have the know-how at our finger-tips? Fertilisation can be brought to barren patches, water supplies can be channelled and conserved and we can produce better wheat and rice than ever before. We know how to preserve the food we have, and the day will surely come when desalination methods will put the resources of the ocean at our disposal and the desert will blossom as the rose. Why pray for bread?

What need is there to pray for healing? We have all the resources of modern medicine. The world's laboratories make new discoveries every day. Yet, in such a seemingly self-sufficient age many are convinced of the evidence of a deepening search for God and a growing conviction of our need of Him, as we realise amid all the violent protest in this modern world that man cannot live by bread alone.

What need is there of the miracles of New Testament days? Miracles are commonplace now as men circle the earth and land on the moon. There seems little beyond the wit of man and, given time, he will be his own saviour! No wonder the Gospel seems irrelevant and has been so diluted that it has not enough strength to meet human need. The strong and manly look to politics and education and technology as the "Open Sesame" to all the treasures of the modern Aladdin's cave.

What need is there for a religious faith when the world seems to make progress without it? True there is another side to the coin. It is easy to deny the need for faith in God, but many who do so break down under the stress of a journey that promises all they desire. Perhaps we do not manage without God as well as we think we do. Some things are hidden from the wise and revealed to the simple. It is not real wisdom to trudge along roads that lead nowhere.

Former roads may seem to have been more meaningful and more of an adventure than the roads we know. Even if they were, it is our fathers who travelled them, not we. Perhaps they were more sure of a destination than we are, or could read their maps with more accuracy than our sketchy glances at the scriptures can. There are still signposts that will guide us aright if we are willing and I believe that many are realising that, after all, we cannot do without a faith that sustains us.

The prompting and the guidance of God is still a reality at which the world may smile, but which faithful men and women find they can trust. Our Lord is still closely involved in every step we take. The Gospel still has something to say, a map to guide and point the way by which we may plan our route—an itinerary that prevents too many wrong turnings.

The Bible is still the world's best-seller; still a guide, thank God, on the road of every day. Here, then, is the source to which we must turn again and again to note that the healing work of our Lord's ministry played no insignificant part. How could it be counted unimportant when He gave so much of His time to a work that was both eternal and personal? Within the rightful calls that were made upon Him to fulfil His Father's purpose He thought it worth while to include so many hours of personal ministry. He healed the sick—a call that we neglect to our hurt—for there can be little doubt that the disciples were sent out on this compassionate work as they proclaimed the kingdom of a Lord who made it possible.

His promise to them was faithfully kept by the gift of a power beyond their own. They knew it—as we should if we were obedient enough. This work was not meant to end with the early Church and there is little doubt that it continued long after His death and resurrection. Research tells us that healing was an integral part of the Church's mission for some three hundred years. It may well have been a normal part of its life up to the point where the Church ceased to be a persecuted minority—in which only the purity of its spirit could keep it alive—and became the recognised faith of the Roman Empire. At the Emperor's word his people became

"Christian" almost overnight and the Church became a popular and fashionable thing, rich and influential for the first time in its history. This sudden influx brought in nothing of the spirit of Christ by which alone the Church can be sustained to do His will.

The period of the Dark Ages found the Church blundering on through a time of unreality and decay, yet God did not leave Himself without witness in this work of healing. In every age some section of the Christian Church, as history shows, has preserved and practised the work of healing through its Lord. Human wisdom is not to be ignored but, in itself, is not enough. Complete dependence upon it denies the possibility of the prompting of the spirit of God in human hearts. It cannot account for the great souls who have changed and transformed the human story in the conviction that they were divinely called.

It may be argued that this is to devalue human knowledge and to rely too much on some vague, inward urge which a man may claim to be the call of God, but in which he might well have been mistaken. There is evidence enough of human error in such things, but we must still beware of the sheer unbelief that denies the validity of the Spirit's prompting simply because we have not known the experience ourselves. A man is wise to act upon an inward certainty that keeps him true to his noblest vision.

In all this there is a sensible and thankful acceptance of all that human intellect and ingenuity make possible for our enrichment. To believe that our Lord meant what He said, as He gave commandment to heal the sick, in no way denies or ignores the tremendous contribution made by medical science. Some tell us that to seek medical aid when we believe in God is a lack of faith. This is nonsense. God Himself needs our help in so many ways. He is not an errand boy who must run to do our bidding and it seems evident that He will not do for us what we can easily do for ourselves. There is a partnership between God and man—and neither is a sleeping partner. God the Creator prepared ore and coal as part of the earth's wealth for man's use but He never made a spade or a mechanical digger. He never made a hypodermic syringe or a supersonic aircraft.

If I run a splinter into my hand I do not pray that God will take it out, for I know how to do it and how to keep the wound clean. If I have a perforated appendix I am grateful for the surgeon who knows how to remove it, and to the theatre staff who keep me from pain and prevent any infection. All healing is of God and we receive it with gratitude and co-operation. Many surgeons will confess that they pray before an operation that God will bless their hands and their skill. For us to give thanks to the Father and to use the skills available to us is not to show any lack of faith but to encourage thankfulness and to acknowledge our partnership with Him.

So we acknowledge all the help that human care and skill can put at our disposal and, at the same time, look to the claims of the Gospel. Advancing human knowledge in no way denies the validity of the ministry of healing prayer, though it is likely that we too readily confuse the miracle with the commonplace. The word "miracle" should be used sparingly. The touch of a switch can flood our room with light or bring us the voices of men walking on the moon. Even this may seem commonplace enough to us, but to some backward race never in touch with the modern world it would be a miracle so unbelievable that it would be frightening. With greater knowledge of spiritual laws we may well see the natural in what now seems miraculous.

A friend whose wife had been healed in our ministry was examined by a specialist who diagnosed cancer in the salivary gland. This caused a swelling in the upper lip which was about the size of a small plum and very painful. An urgent need for an operation was explained to him. He came some sixteen miles to the Vestry Hour and received a ministry at about 8.45 that night. His journey home proved painful in the extreme and he was aware of a change taking place in the upper lip and face. Late that night he telephoned to say that the swelling had gone down and the pain eased. The growth was now reduced to the size of a pea and although it had been adherent to the tissue, it was now moveable in a kind of sac. The next day he reported to the hospital for the operation and the only need was a small incision to remove the "pea". You may doubt that this was cancer, but the surgeon was convinced enough of his diagnosis to treat him with radium needles and a stay in hospital. He is still well as I write—some eleven years after his healing.

A miracle? Some would call it that, but may it not be a "natural" thing to happen, in moments all too rare, when we are ready for the touch of Christ to be upon us? It is when God can make an entrance into these human lives of ours as we open them in faith that the impossible becomes commonplace. We must never give up hoping and trusting in a Lord who healed the sick as part of the redemptive purpose of God.

It may well be true that there is no stage where we

must give up hope of healing or of the touch of Christ, for even in death itself we may see the perfect healing in the faith that our Lord never lets us go from His care. Certainly we can never be absolutely sure that our loved ones cannot be healed in spite of human experience that says otherwise.

A woman who travelled in quiet faith to my Vestry Hour and was healed as she journeyed home telephoned the request that I visit her husband in hospital some fifty miles away. He had suffered some kind of stroke when abroad on business and after some delay had been flown home. Some use had returned to an arm that was paralysed, but the leg had not responded and too long a time had passed for any likely recovery. Some of the patients and members of the staff shared with us in a quiet act of prayer. There was no apparent improvement towards healing, but about twenty minutes after I left the ward to continue my journey some movement came back to his leg. The day came when he could walk, albeit with a slight limp, and was able to go back to work. He and his wife frequently made the fifty-mile journey to take part in the Prayer Fellowship at my church.

A miracle?—or the "natural" thing to happen when the healing Lord enters a human situation to be received in faith? It was natural in Jesus to seek His Father's help and not to doubt that re-creative power was available in Him. See the confidence He brought to His dealings with those in need. This unruffled serenity is evident when He healed Jairus's daughter. The father anxiously urged Him to hurry, but Jesus was delayed and hindered by the crowd and by a woman who pushed her way through to touch the hem of His cloak.

This act of faith on her part deserved attention and, in spite of the need elsewhere, Jesus quietly dealt with that hindrance and made use of it. A woman was healed.

I wonder how many hindrances and frustrating delays could be turned to fruitful opportunities, had we something of the spirit and faith of our Lord. Jairus's fears were apparently well-founded, for the news came that his daughter had died. Now see the calm confidence of the Lord. He told the mourners to keep quiet and cleared everyone from the room except James and John and the girl's parents. It is not helpful to have a negative atmosphere when praying for the sick. Jesus knew that most of the people there had already made up their minds that nothing could be done, so He turned them from the room. Taking the girl by the hand He said, "Get up, child." See how practical He was! In the sheer wonder of that moment of her healing, and knowing the excitement that would follow, He quietly told the parents to give her something to eat.

Jesus knew the secret that we find so elusive, the secret of perfect trust in the Father. He did not rely on the capricious whim of a God who, for some inscrutable reason of His own, decided whether or not to help. God is always ready to help. There is an air of unreality about prayer if that truth is in doubt. It was doubted by His own people in the town where He was brought up, and so He could not do many mighty works there. They had known Him as a boy, known His father and mother and the family. How could *He* hope to heal the sick or even claim to be a teacher worth listening to?

The secret that Jesus knew was that He could expect an answer to prayer that was a vital link between

Himself and His Father's power. To be confidently expectant keeps prayer vitally alive. Not that we should be cock-sure or take God for granted, for that would be self-reliant. Be confident enough to rely upon God and on the partnership He asks of us.

Confidence and humility make good partners as we learn of the Christ who is on the familiar roads of today. Times have changed, but He has not. There is so much more available for human good in our age than in the days of Jesus and we are grateful for so many advances in human knowledge. We can be thankful for material discoveries without being blind to the need to adventure in the realms of the spirit. God has yet more light and truth to make clear to seeking minds and hearts, and it has been said that the great discoveries of the next half-century will be in the realms of the spiritual.

Certainly we have much to learn about prayer and the laws of prayer—a realm in which we can be blindly ignorant. We should bring every gift of heart and intellect to this task. For one thing, we must learn the need of our acceptance of what God would give us. In some things the Father can give only as we are ready to receive. *Give* is the operative word, for we can never *earn* His grace, and every gift involves at least two people—the one who gives and the one who receives. "Why does not God do something?" is often a cry of despair, and we forget that there are some things that God will not do without our help. Some question the need for prayer when God already knows our need. They argue that prayer can make no difference, for God will do what He wants to do anyway. Of course prayer is not an attempt to get God to change His mind or do us some special favour because we deserve it. We have no need to jog God's memory in case He has forgotten what we asked Him yesterday.

Prayer is partly instinctive and should be a natural activity. It is quiet and confident fellowship with God and a glad partnership that opens the way for His spirit to fill us. It is an admission that we rely upon Him. It is in this realm of practical prayer that the disciplines of a prayer group take on a new significance. To pray together can bring us to a common mind about the many things we need to be sure about. For most of us it is true that, in fellowship, we can better discover the mind of Christ and know the leading of His spirit that challenges all we do.

We live in a world such as the disciples never dreamed about, in which the local situation is always coloured by that wider view of the world's needs that makes our own seem so puny. Yet the Christ must be seen to be relevant to our local situation. To look lovingly at our fellows' need, yet see the vastness of that need, can be discouraging. We can but do what is to be done within the limits of the conditions we know. How urgent is the need to take Christ at His word, remembering that He too was once limited by His manhood and was never able to reach all who needed Him in that short ministry on earth.

It is here, in the place where life has set us, that we must be ready to co-operate with the Lord of the whole world. On our own road we must travel steadfastly with our eye upon Him, so that we ignore the signposts that point to an easier or a shorter way. Every road on which we walk is a road of opportunity where dreams can be realised in a partnership that makes us part of His eternal purpose.

It has always been in a climate of unbelief that the

world's great souls have made their finest contribution. A discouraging feature of the age in which we live is in the apparent absence of impact by the Christian Church. Many churches close their doors. Too many, in my view, have given up too soon under the pressures of those who talk of the church as if it were a cinema or a golf club that must be shut down if it doesn't pay. It is a heartbreak to see our buildings, once the beloved Bethels of our fathers, so lovingly and hopefully built, now turned into bingo halls and warehouses. True, city centre redevelopment and the movement of population have made the closure of many churches inevitable, but we should remember that God once raised up a Wesley when things were infinitely worse. Do you think God has given up because of the climate of the age in which we live? Has He no more ideas? Can He not still use men and women who gather in fellowship with Him and claim His promised presence?

Modern roads may seem bare of the excitement and adventure of former days, but we must see again that adventure is within the heart and spirit of man—not in the circumstances of his day. There are discouragements enough in these days when so many break under the stress of modern life, but discoveries of the Healing Christ can still be made. Listen to a young woman who met her Lord and who finishes her story with the thought, "I shudder to think what would have happened to me had I never known the healing of Jesus." The account that follows is in her own words with slight editorial omissions.

"I first met the Rev. Bert Jordan in 1966. I was then on the verge of a nervous breakdown and had seen a psychiatrist, though the thought of doing so frightened me. I refused to go into hospital. Tablets were prescribed but my condition grew worse and it was at this time that I met my mother's minister, Mr Jordan. She had told him of my condition and asked for my name to be included in his prayer-healing list. He did more than that, for he came to see me in the village where I lived and visited me at home. I was greatly comforted by that visit and arranged to have a further ministry on the following Saturday at the Vestry Hour. After a number of weekly ministries I recovered and was able to resume work in a busy office. I enjoyed good health for two years and then suffered a more serious breakdown, brought on by a series of events, but mainly the pressure of work. I could not explain the torture of this breakdown. I wanted to die yet was afraid of death. The pain in my head was unbearable and I cried day and night.

"The ministries I received then were a blessing indeed, for nothing else would relieve the pain in my head. I feared that I had a tumour on the brain. My doctor insisted that I go into a psychiatric hospital. On the morning I was to be admitted I begged my husband to ask the minister to come in as I needed a ministry that would help me to face either life or death. (At this point I felt I was dying and was cold and had no strength.) Mr Jordan arrived at 9 a.m. and ministered to me and it was then I knew I would get well, for I felt the closeness of God and knew that He cared. Three weeks in hospital with visits in which I received the laying-on-of-hands, and I was well again. The psychiatrist admitted that the ministries of prayer had played a great part in my swift recovery."

The Lord of the New Testament is alive and active on the roads of today. To see Him compassionately aware of human need, to believe in Him, as One who is not only willing to help but also able to do so in ways beyond the world's understanding, is to face with new hope the challenges of our twentieth-century journey and see again the "miracles" of the commonplace. The greatest discovery a man can make is that, on the roads of today, he may meet the Master who walked and healed in Galilee so long ago.

9

THE ROAD OF PARTNERSHIP

MANY AND VARIED are the roads on which men and women have discovered the living Lord. He invites us into partnership. This may sound presumptuous but it in no way denies His Lordship or our discipleship. The sheer wonder of it will keep us in this relationship of master and servant in spite of His word that He will call us friends. To think again of those New Testament roads thrills us with the possibilities of such a confrontation, and its challenge, becoming part of our experience on the road of today. Cling to that truth, that we are not called to an impossible task, but to a partnership in which we can rely upon a Divine Companion.

Without the faith that Jesus is alive and active in human affairs, we need go no further, for the Church's ministry of healing presupposes this to be true. This ministry is not therefore limited to a humanitarian attempt to bring comfort and understanding to our fellows. It is a conviction, strengthened by experience, that His touch still has its ancient power.

A woman with two teenage daughters and a helpful and happy family life experienced a steady increase in faith as ministries continued. She had spinal trouble which gave her considerable pain as the spine would tighten and become as rigid as a poker. A ministry of the laying-on-of-hands brought immediate relief, and in a few minutes the spine was supple and free from pain.

Days later the pain returned and complete healing seemed elusive. This condition, among others from which she was finally healed, kept her far from well for a long time. Her own words speak little of her patient seeking, but tell of her healing.

"Pain in my back and neck continued for some months and was diagnosed as arthritis. Treatment was prescribed which the doctor said would ease the pain but not effect a cure, and I would need to live with it. After months of suffering I sought a ministry from my minister, the Rev. Bert Jordan. When he put his hands upon me in prayer, I felt a warmth circulate through my whole body and a definite relief from pain. I made regular visits to the Vestry Hour and received some ministries at home and in this period the pain grew less. On one occasion as a ministry was received, I felt a peculiar sensation in my back as though something had 'given'. The next day I awoke to realise that I had no pain at all and have had no recurrence of the trouble and have been entirely free from pain."

* * * *

See how far we have travelled on New Testament roads:

The Damascus Road—with its challenges to our faith and our thinking, and sometimes a challenge to the very direction we are taking. Here is the road where we are brought face to face with truth that we have tried to ignore or to kick against. Here we learn, for the insistent Christ makes it plain, that we cannot forever close our minds to the truth or our ears to its challenge. We dare not ignore forever the Holy Spirit's prompting.

The Emmaus Road—convinces us that the Christ broke

from His tomb on Easter Day and is loose in the world again. We need that conviction, as Cleopas and his friend needed it, for we are familiar with the heartbreak road on which we want to give up and go home. Our hearts have burned within us as the truth has been made plain and we have recognised the "Stranger" who walked with us. It is on this road that what we have longed to believe is discovered to be true. A road of renewed hopes, where the temptation to go home has been changed to a determination to travel back to the Jerusalem of new adventures.

The Jericho Road—is the road on which we see more clearly our fellows' need, and reach out to help. A road on which the need becomes obvious and the challenge of it grips us. On this road, too, we may feel that we are just one of the crowd yet have part in the healing of some Bartimaeus. Where others impatiently say, "Keep quiet!" we discover faith enough to say to those in need, "Take heart, stand up, He is calling you."

The Road to the Temple—challenges us within the Christian Church to look again at its work and witness. The Servant Church is set in a community and in a world that is to be served. We may give generously of our silver and gold, but that is not all we have to give. We have partnership with the Christ who can set a man upon his feet. The challenge is that we should make up our minds about this ministry in which human need can be so wonderfully met; the challenge to be unashamed to proclaim the Healing Christ and claim His promised power.

The Road of Assurance—is travelled only by the grace of God. We travel its miles in faith as we watch the Christ at work in the New Testament and see for ourselves His compassionate power that still enriches those who seek Him. This road keeps our faith alive and keeps us faithful to our tasks. Its certainties sustain us in a climate of doubt—a great need in an age that placards the virtues of self-sufficiency.

The Road of Today—is the road where we are and on which we see that truth passed on from the Christ of history is relevant to our own experience. The impact of the first century is seen to impinge upon the twentieth as the unchanging Lord walks at our side. The life and death, the ministry and the resurrection are seen, not as isolated events in time but as part of eternal truth. It is still a pioneer road, for the frontiers have not been reached. We do not inherit the Christian faith, though its tenets may be passed down the years, for each of us needs to experience for ourselves that which makes the faith live in us. The Master we follow is not some noble figure of history but the Lord of the everyday.

So we come to the *Road of Partnership* where practical issues are made plain and must be faced if we are to know a partnership that tells of our Lord's need of us. Be reminded of the old legend of our Lord returning to heaven after His earthly ministry, and being asked by the archangel Gabriel, "What plans have you made for the continuation of your work on earth?" Jesus replied, "I have Peter and John and the others; I have Mary and Martha and the other women. They will tell others and the work will go on." But Gabriel wasn't satisfied. "Lord, supposing Peter is too busy with his fishing and the women too concerned with household duties and do not pass your message on, what other plans have you?" The legend tells us that Jesus said simply, "I have no other plans."

God has left so much for us to do. We may doubt His wisdom in trusting us so much, but it seems to be His way. There is a partnership between the Lord and those who will serve Him. Our response in faith opens the sluice gates and lets His grace and power through. The need is obvious, for men cry out for certainties and we see that our Lord entrusts us with such unsearchable riches. There are practical steps that can be taken as we make response to challenges that are obvious enough. There is much that we can do, and one practical step is for Christian men and women to pray together.

Prayer groups can be formed when two or three are prepared to meet together with their Lord, seek His guidance, and make an honest search for the truth of His call to partnership. Every journey begins with a single step, and this may well be the step to take. Get together in a questioning attitude if need be, learn together of the strength that soon comes to a group with a common purpose, and remember that you will not be alone but in the presence of a Lord who keeps His promise. If you ask the question, "What is the Church's ministry of healing, and what part can the ordinary Christian play in it?"—you will not be the first to make such an enquiry. There is an evident movement of the Spirit of God in this growing interest in prayerful outreach. We ought not to leave its possibilities unexplored nor bring to our searching anything less than an honest commitment.

This will soon prove to be a practical and rewarding exercise of Christian fellowship. Partnership is the operative word—it must be, for we shall soon be led to so much that we cannot possibly do alone. There are exciting discoveries to be made within such a group of earnest people who set out to assess the implications of the New Testament commission to preach the gospel and *heal the sick.* If such a commission is genuine and was not meant to end with the Apostolic era, then the modern Church is called to seek, with faith and humility, a deeper and more profound understanding of the Gospel's full mission to this age.

Turn it down if you will—but not before you have given yourself to a prayerful and disciplined investigation, and come to an honest judgement. Remember that great discoveries in prayer are made by men and women who expect much from God, and are ready to give much to Him. Such a group will soon be very sure of the Lord's nearness, and assurance will be undoubted as ministry in prayer sees burdens lifted, and men and women healed and blessed in a work done in partnership with Christ.

Every situation of health or sickness has within it a factor that involves a man's spirit—his real self. Religious belief is always involved, for it is true that what a man believes (or does not believe) deep down, whether or not he is aware of it, affects the whole of him. The Christian faith is concerned with man's wholeness—and so it should be, for its Lord is concerned about it too. It is obvious that a sick body, maybe pain-ridden and limited, can affect the sufferer's mind and spirit. It is not always so obvious, but is nevertheless true, that a man who is sick in soul cannot be "healthy" though his body may not yet show symptoms of ill-health. To be fearful and anxious, or to be eaten up with bitter resentment, will have its inevitable effect. We are not machines that sometimes need an engineer's repair job, but personalities of soul and mind and body in constant need of the Creator's hand upon us.

A Christian prayer group becomes a therapeutic agency as compassion and faith enrich its sense of caring. It is a common experience to feel this atmosphere where men and women meet in love to pray for the needs of others. Begun in prayer and saturated in prayer, the very room takes on the spirit of calm assurance. This is therapy indeed to those who enter for healing for themselves or others.

In one of my pastorates, fire destroyed the Church Hall and classrooms. We rebuilt on a more ambitious scale and the new building included a small but beautiful sanctuary dedicated for use in the healing ministry. The sanctuary was placed at one corner of the new buildings so that it could be separately entered and left open all day for private prayer. The foundations had been dug and I went down to the site one morning before work began and, with a handful of workmen gathered around, laid the first brick. We prayed, standing in the rain, for God's blessing upon the use to which the sanctuary would be put. From the very first there was a feeling of peace within that little place. Workmen who came later and knew nothing of our prayers as the building was begun confessed to a strange sense of peace as they worked within its walls.

Some of the healings recorded in these pages took place within this sanctuary. We need have no doubt of the very atmosphere of healing as we meet in the fellowship of prayer. Regularity of meeting is important in a prayer group. How often a group can meet depends upon circumstances, but make sure it is regular. This brings a sense of "oneness" in fellowship and purpose that cannot be achieved by spasmodic attendance. Loyalty is more important than numbers. Chairs set in a semi-circle add to the sense of fellowship and sharing, especially when discussion is encouraged. None of us achieves the ideal, but it is good to have a room just big enough for the group, as too large a room will not encourage the shy to take part.

To study together, to receive the help of each other's insights, to question and share intimately in Christian experience, can help to clear the mists of doubt and misunderstanding. Everything that is done in the group is then seen in perspective, and seen as part of the whole purpose of bringing men and women into the healing presence of Christ. It will be helpful in the early days of a group to alternate study and discussion with a devotional act of worship in which teaching plays a part. Such meetings come effectively to a climax when prayers are offered for the sick. The quiet ministry of the laying-on-of-hands becomes a natural and fitting ending to an hour spent in compassionate concern. In each case where I have introduced the healing ministry to my churches, we have begun with study and discussion and then changed to meetings of a more devotional pattern. The value of study is undoubted, but, having come to a common mind about the aims of the fellowship, a devotional act has led us more surely to the moment of prayer for the sick.

A prayer list should be prepared and kept carefully up-to-date. If this is not done it will not be meaningful for long. One method is to have a notebook and pen available so that members can enter new names as they arrive. Another method is to ask the group to state such names verbally and tell briefly of the need. A duplicated list of those whom we would remember in prayer, available to each member of the group and used daily by them, is a great advantage. It may be wise to agree that names should be included on the prayer list only by request of the sick person or a member of the group. No confidences must be broken and some prefer to use only Christian names.

Prayer time should come towards the end of the group meeting when the names on the prayer list may be read aloud by the leader. If the list is a long one, several names should be read between short periods of silent prayer. I find it useful to alternate this method of reading names aloud with the practice of each member looking at his own list while prayer is in the silence. A short time spent, before prayers, in reviewing the list and giving news of those we pray for is a helpful way of keeping the list "alive".

Friendliness and the personal touch is vital in establishing relationships. Newcomers should be welcomed and introduced to the group. An experienced group finds it natural to set a welcoming atmosphere in which the visitor quickly feels relaxed and at ease. It is good to stay for conversation after each meeting is formally closed so that introductions can be made and confidence fostered. The prayer list should be used daily in private prayer and a minister will be grateful for the knowledge that his people uphold him daily as he goes about his pastoral duties. He will know a strange—or maybe not so strange!—sense of strength in his awareness of his people's prayers.

At all cost the prayer group must avoid the error of feeling apart from the life of the church. It has its own work to do and its own disciplines to undertake, but it must never give the impression of being "superior" to the other work so lovingly done by other departments of the church. You may be a useful member of a prayer group but utterly inadequate to teach in Junior Church or run a youth club. Such a group will most surely be leaven in the lump, but must have no undue pride in a task in which the triple virtues of humility, faith and compassion will undoubtedly influence the whole body of the church.

* * * *

THE VESTRY HOUR

This is an hour (or longer, as the need dictates) when the minister is available in his vestry to minister to the sick and troubled. Those most in need of help do not easily come to the minister's home, in spite of the warm welcome the manse or the vicarage may offer. People generally find it easier to come to a church building, where they feel it to be less of an intrusion on a minister's own time. As such an hour becomes a familiar part of the church's programme it will be seen to give opportunity to share confidentially with someone who will listen with sympathy and understanding. This in itself is worth the effort and the time spent, but a minister has something more to give in the name of his Lord. There is a power in his prayers as he ministers in the faith that the promises of the Gospel are real. It is a privilege and a humbling experience to share his people's confidence and to bring them and their needs to the promised resources of the Divine Healer.

It will soon be demonstrated that such a Vestry Hour with its quiet, confident ministry, is wider in scope than would at first seem likely. Many from outside his own

Church will value the opportunity of pastoral help from a man whose attitude and confidence speak of his own quiet certainties. The Church's work is widened and denominational barriers break down as confidence grows. In this more personal ministry, as in the work of the group, regularity is an important factor.

A waiting-room of suitable size is an asset, and a receptionist needs to be carefully chosen. In my own case I am fortunate enough to be able to leave this duty to my wife, whose quiet serenity and relaxed attitude sets the right atmosphere for those awaiting a ministry. The receptionist gives a welcome and puts visitors at ease and keeps the conversation on the right level so that the period of waiting is free from the doctor's surgery type of symptom-sharing. As a matter of fact there are few dull moments in my waiting-room, for the accent is on fellowship and caring—and often on humour. Many are thus able to relax before coming to the vestry for prayer. An "Engaged" sign on the vestry door is useful so that no disturbance distracts at the moment of ministry. If there is a telephone on the premises it is better in another room.

Another advantage in setting aside some special time for interviews of this kind is that both minister and people have opportunity to prepare for it. Needless to say, as far as possible the ministrant will be calm and assured as he comes to such an hour. He will need to be relaxed and quiet in spirit. Life rushes us a bit sometimes, and it is not always possible to have a free moment or two as we come from some other duty to this one. Even so, it is a wonderful experience to be able to come so quickly into the presence of Christ and let Him minister to us before we minister to others in His name. Ideally, I suppose, we should have a time of quiet preparation, but in a busy life this is not always possible immediately before the Vestry Hour begins. It is profoundly moving to discover that God understands our need and His grace is sufficient to bring us from the busyness of life into the calm of His presence.

PREPARING FOR A MINISTRY

When it is known in advance that someone is seeking help for the first time, I find that an interview at an appointed time is helpful. It gives sufficient time to share thoughts and to make clear what this ministry is all about. A sense of haste—which can so easily intrude when the waiting-room is crowded—is not so helpful to newcomers who need time to feel relaxed and quietly ready. Those who come for a ministry should give thought to what they are about to do. They should pray about it and prepare themselves as helpfully as they can, so that this appointment with their Lord is acknowledged in a spirit of expectancy and hope. True enough, no minister can give himself to this exacting work if he is unsure that God can use him, but few will realise its possibilities or its worth until they are ready to be obedient and humble enough not to be afraid of failure.

There should be no embarrassment in asking for healing prayers. Why should there be, when we are urged to pray for one another? We must certainly not leave prayer out of our reckoning until every other method has failed. It is far better to come to God in expectant faith than to come in sheer desperation. If you are ill, send for the doctor. Accept, with gratitude to him and to God, the skills and knowledge your doctor can bring to the task of making you well. There may be a time when someone comes to the limit of medical help and nothing more can humanly be done, but why wait for that point before sharing your need with God? Pray for your doctor as he treats you. You and he and God are partners in a very real sense and you impoverish that partnership if you leave God out. Seek the help of your minister or your fellow Christians, for they have a concern for your well-being.

Do make some preparation of spirit when you seek the ministry of prayer and never come lightly into the presence of the Creator. You will rightly expect the one who ministers to you to be prepared in heart and mind, and we have already seen that he may well be a busy man. He will need your prayers. No moment of worship, or of such intimacy with God, should be sought without the best preparation we can make for such a privilege. Relax, and in the quietness let the spirit of God fill you. If you wait some days for a pre-arranged ministry, see to it that each day has some moment set aside in quiet and expectant waiting upon God. You are asking Him to fill you with healing grace—ask also that you may be ready to receive it.

Such preparation will enable you to approach the moment of ministry with confidence as well as gratitude. Do not be afraid to hope for healing, and do not bring your doubts with you or burden yourself unduly with demands for "proof". This is not to suggest that you should be credulous or unreasoning, but simply to remember that you cannot apply to the realm of the spiritual the same "proof" tests that may well apply in other spheres. This is an act of faith. Never childish, but always child-like. The blind man whom Jesus healed had no idea how He did it, or even who He was. It is not "knowing all the answers" that will enable God to heal you—but a faith that believes it possible.

THE LAYING-ON-OF-HANDS

Still on the road of partnership, we think of our Lord's commission to "lay hands upon the sick". Much has been written about this act of healing and we need not spend too long with it. Certainly it is a solemn act of faith that must never be glibly talked about or carelessly done. It has been used through the ages as a priestly act of blessing. It would seem to be a spontaneous gesture of compassionate sharing of another's need and a longing to help. Those who feel led to minister in this way know its worth, for when prayerfully administered it brings more than a human touch. In this way the charismatic gift of healing is passed to the one receiving the ministry. If there is such a gift in my hands I thank God for it and will gladly use it as He commands. Apart from such a charismatic gift in the individual, I believe that this gift is given to the Church and that many would use it if they were aware of it. How shall we discover such a gift in ourselves or in the Church, save by coming to that faithful moment when we are obedient enough to use it?

No one with any experience of the laying-on-of-hands will deny that it brings a feeling of warmth or coolness, according to the need of the one ministered to. It is often described to me as a mild electric shock which is very pleasant. As I have ministered by laying hands on an arthritic joint, for example, it has been described as being very like the heat treatment of hospital therapy, but it lasts much longer, maybe twenty-four hours or more. On the other hand, when ministering to someone with a high temperature, my hands have burned like fire and so has the patient's head, yet when the ministry is finished it is said, "How cooling your hands were."

That Jesus laid His hands upon the sick would not give us any right to do so had He not expressly commanded that His disciples should continue to heal as they preached the kingdom. Experience convinces us of its worth as, in His name and by this ministry, pain is frequently relieved, stiff joints move freely and sleep is often induced. The healing of wounds is sometimes accelerated. I have known a leg ulcer some two inches across that resisted healing for twelve months—healed in a week after prayer.

It is commonplace for anxiety and tension and fear to respond to healing prayer. The very fact of sharing with our Lord in this intimate way and being assured of His concern is a comfort, but He promises more than comfort. Keep on this road of partnership. It is the ancient and modern road on which men and women have known the enrichment of a Divine Companion. It is a road of obedience and humility, a road of compassion and discovery—for on this road we find how true it is that the Lord will use us as He used His disciples so long ago.

10

THE ROAD OF EXPERIENCE

NOTHING CAN DENY the Gospel records their rightful place as the source of the Christian faith, for in them we have not only the written account of our Lord's life and work and resurrection but also the promise of our Lord to be with us still. What happened in Palestine in a little, despised corner of the Roman Empire so long ago cannot be confined to the first century. It is an event that continues through the ages with a living Christ who is contemporary with His people of every generation. The experiences that sent the apostles on their mammoth task of preaching and healing take on a new relevance as they become our own. Thank God for every road that leads us to faithful discipleship, and especially for the road of personal experience on which *we* meet that same Lord.

Those who have known the renewing power of Christ in healing can say so with conviction. I pray that many who have not known Him so intimately may be led to discover Him in these pages. None can so surely convince another of the truth of this ministry as one who has been convinced by experience. This final chapter seeks to supplement what has already been said as some to whom I have had the privilege to minister tell of its results in their own words. They can testify to its worth.

Not all who seek healing come with an assured faith

and it cannot be expected that they should. It is quite wrong to put the onus on their faith, in a way that suggests blame because of their lack if healing does not come. The Church's ministry of healing is not faith healing and should never be so called. It is God's healing—a gift and a commission given to His Church and His people. It is not the faith that we bring to it that heals, but the power of God. This in no way denies the value of faith or the fact that it can be so helpful a factor in healing.

Faith has a part that we are wise not to underestimate, for it helps us to accept what God has to give, and we have seen how needful this acceptance is. We must not say that faith is *always* demanded of those to whom we minister in prayer. We may pray for a young child who would not be expected to bring any sense of expectancy to the act or make it an act of faith. We could minister to someone who is unconscious and cannot take any active part at all in what we do. Sometimes in "absent healing" the sick person may have no knowledge of our prayers. True, we ought to seek healing prayer-help with all the faith and trust that we can bring to our request, but always remember that the source of our healing is in God's response and our acceptance.

A member of my prayer group who was trained in nursing was in a maternity ward awaiting the arrival of her baby. She was admitted to hospital before the baby was due because of some trouble in a former pregnancy. A fellow patient in the ward was so ill that she was not expected to recover and the mother-to-be went quietly to the hospital chapel each morning to pray for the woman's healing. She said nothing about her prayers to anyone, but after a day or two the sick woman asked her where she went each morning—did she go to church? This was admitted, and the patient said, "I felt sure you did, for I have felt a strange sense of peace and assurance each time you go for which I cannot account, unless you have prayed for me." In telling this story the ex-nurse said that, in spite of her training which made her well aware of the other's serious condition, she remembered that she was a member of our prayer and healing fellowship and could not deny that with God all things are possible. Professionally cautious, she prayed positively, and her prayer was answered.

There was no active faith on the part of the patient, for at first she was not aware that she was being prayed for. The faith was in the heart of the ex-nurse who prayed so lovingly despite the odds against her faith. We must never insist upon a technique that puts too much emphasis on human effort and not enough on the compassionate power of God. Many make the discovery of a healing Lord through the evidence of experience. "Whereas I was blind, now I see."

It is not at all easy to overcome human anxiety when the need is deep, and many never reach the point when they lean all their weight upon Christ. If *complete* faith was essential, then maybe few of us would be helped, for we come to our Lord with hesitation and some reservation. Yet, if we say that He can use and strengthen the faith we bring, this is not to excuse our own lack, but to acknowledge the graciousness of the Father who tempers the wind to the shorn lamb. To have a series of ministries at a weekly Vestry Hour gives opportunity for a quiet building of faith and trust.

Both a pre-arranged Vestry Hour and the spontaneous pastoral visit give opportunity, in different ways, to come into the presence of our Lord. It is not always so easy in hospital now that visiting hours are extended and the wards full of visitors. Most hospital staffs are helpful when the visiting minister asks for the privacy of the bedside screen. Where the staff is sympathetic and when, in a small ward, the other patients are willing to share what is being done, the experience of a ministry can be enriching indeed. It is useful to make arrangements to visit for this purpose at some agreed time. This acknowledges the skill and care of the medical staff and a faith in the healing Lord, in a partnership that can often be wonderfully blessed. I was once called to visit a famous hospital to minister to the wife of a friend. The patient who made this request was an ex-ward sister, skilled enough to be aware of her own condition. Another patient in the two-bedded ward, a much older woman who was gravely ill, requested a ministry when I arrived. Both husbands were present. The following is taken from a tape-recording made some years after the event.

"In April 1958 I underwent a breast amputation in the . . . Hospital, following which I had a severe haemorrhage for three weeks. Despite all treatment, it was not arrested and my husband asked the ward sister if the Rev. Bert Jordan might come in that evening to minister to me in prayer. She readily agreed and I and another patient received the ministry of the laying-on-of-hands. Both of us had cancer, but how wonderfully God used our minister that night! My haemorrhage stopped there and then, and within a few days, to everyone's astonishment, I was able to leave hospital. The other patient, after a second operation for abdominal obstruction, which had not proved successful, had tubes in her stomach and bladder and a saline drip in her leg. She also received a ministry and that night was greatly improved. The tubes were removed and she was soon out of hospital. She got about again quite happily, but many months later she died suddenly and peacefully. In God's grace she had been saved untold suffering."

Such a variety of truth can be learned on the road of experience—not all concerned with healing in the accepted sense. Situations can be transformed in a way that brings a sense of wonder as we realise the power of Jesus to bring health and reconciliation. He is concerned with every aspect of human life, for health is such a wide term that it takes in the whole of our experience. It may be true that physical healing seems more spectacular, but a quiet healing of a troubled situation can bring equal joy.

Unhappy relationships bring strain and dis-ease and can be stubbornly wearing. A good many break down under the strain of constant friction at work or at home and we would be wise to realise that here, too, is a sphere into which the Christ can bring reconciling grace. It is commonplace enough to see the strain that can come into a home where one member of the family suffers such breakdown. It can be a vicious circle, of circumstances causing breakdown, and the breakdown in turn aggravating the situation. Other members of the family do not always understand the problems of the one afflicted and often give the cruel advice, "Pull yourself together!"

How desperately the healing and reconciling Lord is needed in situations where human personalities clash and bring distress—and how often He remains uninvited! A psychiatrist, with his patient's permission, referred her to the ministry of prayer in my church. He had treated her in hospital for a couple of years or so, during which time she had alternated between being resident and an out-patient. She had been married for several years and had no children, which was a sorrow to both her and her husband. She seemed unable to cope with the responsibilities of the home and there was danger of the marriage breaking down. It was not the easiest of situations, but eventually we got wife and husband together to share in a ministry in which they sought to accept Christ's healing and reconciling grace. The situation was healed and apart from occasional check-ups the wife never returned for further treatment.

There is perhaps nothing to equal the road of personal experience to convince us of the worth of this ministry. To be sure of the touch of our Lord upon us or upon our loved ones is to be made aware of a re-creative grace and power that we had not even imagined to be possible. It is a great adventure to welcome Him into the common affairs of daily life and learn of His caring interest, in which nothing seems too trivial for His concern.

Friendships are wonderfully cemented in the sharing of another's need and in the sharing of deep certainties. Some to whom we have ministered through the years lose touch, but many keep contact and their friendship and encouragement sustains the work as it continues and widens. There are those who remind us of the moment when we stood together in some grim need, and discovered it to be a moment of healing as our Lord surrounded us with love and power. I think of a young married woman who was deputy organist at one of my churches. She lives a busy life in the world of music and is a talented singer and organist. She tells of her turning to the Lord in need and of His gracious response.

"There have been three occasions when the ministry of prayer has been such a help to me. Soon after my second little girl was born, a neighbour would insist on being in my home so often and for so long that it hindered my work each day. This made me tense to such an extent that I often broke down and cried when anyone spoke to me. A coffee evening for the church was held at my home and a woman, who had herself received healing, suggested that I ask the minister to pray with me. When everyone had gone the Rev. Bert Jordan and his wife stayed behind and I received the ministry of prayer as he laid his hands upon me. I was made quite well and able to cope.

"On another occasion I had received treatment for a slipped disc. Manipulative treatment seemed to put things right but, reaching for some shopping in the car next day, I slipped the disc again. Mr Jordan rang my home on another matter and, hearing of my pain, paid me a visit. A quiet prayer first and then he laid his hand on my spine. It is difficult to describe the sensation one feels when having a ministry. It seems as if the whole body is made lighter and the pain is lifted away. But more than the pain this time, for the disc went back into place and I have been all right since then.

"The third experience resulted from an accident in the garden. I bruise very easily and when part of a sawn-off tree trunk fell and hit me just below the knee, I almost fainted with the pain of it. This happened at eleven o'clock in the morning and I was due to play for a funeral service in two hours and did not know how I would manage. Arriving at the church in good time, I received a ministry in the vestry. The pain was banished at once and, to my amazement, my leg did not swell or bruise. The graze below my knee quickly healed."

Physical healings are not the only product of this ministry which can also bring an uplift of spirit. A woman who knew much pain for some ten years had lengthy treatment for osteo-arthritis in spine and neck. One shoulder was affected so that she could not raise her arm very high. She had several ministries which brought relief from pain and then, during prayer, she felt something "give" in her shoulder and she was able to move her arm freely. There has been continued freedom from pain, and arm and neck remain supple. Everyone who knows her agrees that she is more alive and vital, and she acknowledges this new attitude of spirit as a great gift from the Healing Christ.

One thing we learn from experience is that our Lord deals with us as individuals, offering, not a general panacea, but a meeting of personal need. A friend was assured by her doctor that she was pregnant. Some months later it was decided to abort what was thought to be a dead foetus. I ministered to her in hospital and we asked that God would come into the situation and that His will might be done. The attempted abortion was *not* successful and she was sent home for a time. During the ministry she felt that two hands were clasped over her abdomen—though at the time my hands were laid on her head. It was discovered later that she had *not* been pregnant when it was first diagnosed but had become so later. This explained why the baby had apparently not grown and was thought to be dead. The baby was duly born and is now a fine schoolgirl, in spite of the advice that it would still have been wise to abort because of the drugs given earlier on.

Someone has said that God goes ahead of us, planting the future with surprises. In this ministry we are often made aware of His gracious foresight and can look back at moments when, although we did not know it, He was with us to bring joy to our years yet to come.

Absent healing is common enough but is not always recognised for what it is. A car accident landed one of my people in hospital, together with her two children. The children were not badly hurt but the mother had a fractured skull and sternum, a wound in her head which needed twenty-seven stitches and an eye that closed with swelling. One child was allowed into the ward when I visited the mother and was very upset that her eye would not open. The ward sister consoled him but said that his mummy's eye would not open for a week. A ministry was given and, to the delight of that little boy, his mother's eye opened freely.

The incident of absent healing came on her return home from hospital. She was told that plastic surgery would be needed on her forehead and she had constant head pains that would not be relieved. We prayed for her within the context of the Sunday evening service. The time was 6.45 p.m. We discovered later that at exactly that time the pain ceased, suddenly and completely. She recovered without the return of pain and without the need for plastic surgery.

Of the many roads we may travel with the Healing Christ, this road of experience is the most reassuring. Some find it at the very beginning of their search. Some find it after disciplined patience. Our great need is to begin the journey with hope. On that road we make discoveries, are confronted with challenges and are often refreshed by the experiences of others. Many have found the healing Lord on the road of despair and disappointment, and then the very direction of their lives is changed. Some find Him on the road to the temple—in the fellowship and worship of the church to which they belong. Some find Him because someone else has found Him and encourages them to take heart.

One thing is certain. He would have us make such discoveries, as He reaches out with compassionate heart and that amazing power made so plain in the Gospels.

Meet Him on the road where you live and be made whole—and give God the glory.